Proven Beyond Doubt

By George Grant Thorogood

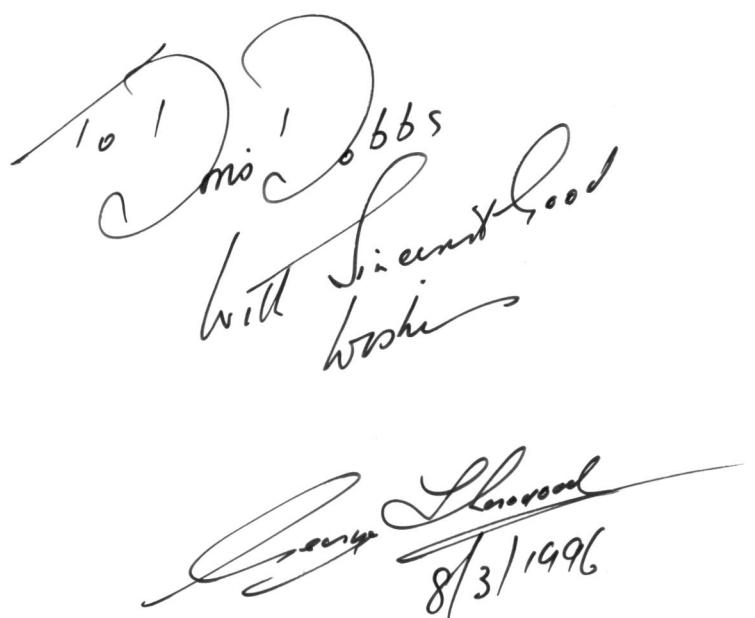

To the people of the Netherlands

Proven Beyond Doubt

As it strikes, it gazes down,
Upon a plot in Uden town,
Where row on row with headstones white
Lie sons and brothers lost in the fight;
The cross of sacrifice its vigil keeps
While the valiant rest in their final sleep.
They came by land, by sea, by sky,
An avenging host, prepared to die,
From lands of Empire and England's shore
O'er the sea as their fathers before;
Girt for battle, people to free,
To liberate them from their misery.
Weapons of war their tools of trade
Wielded as like a sharpened blade
But always in war a price is paid,
For in their thousands in earth were laid.
A young life given, forever lost,
Was the price, the tragic cost.
Over the years the pilgrims came
To stand just briefly with sons of fame,
To remember a loved one's smiling face,
Recalling moments of joy and grace.
But as the clock extends the years
Their numbers dwindle, there are fewer tears.
But beloved by those they came to free,
In whose care they will always be,
The torch of remembrance is held in hand
By the noble people of the Netherland

George Grant Thorogood

Published 1995 by Thorogood Publications
91 Ventnor Road, Solihull, B92 9BH, England

© 1995 George Grant Thorogood
ISBN 0 9525394 03

All rights reserved
No part of this publication may be reproduced
in any form or by any means without permission

British Library Cataloguing in Publication Data
A catalogue record for this book is available from the British Library

Printed in England by Short Run Press Limited

Contents

PREFACE ix

INTRODUCTION. xi

DUTY CALLS 1

A ONE WAY JOURNEY 11

TO LAY THE GHOST. 33

MORE DUTCH HOSPITALITY 61

IN SEARCH OF THE FACTS 81

COMMEMORATION DAYS IN NOORD BRABANT. 105

THE FINAL TRIBUTE 127

BIBLIOGRAPHY 140

APPENDICES 141

Preface

IN THE SPRING OF 1989 I RECEIVED A LETTER FROM A DUTCHMAN BY THE name of Ad Hermans, who lives in the town of Geldrop in the Netherlands. He enquired if I were the brother of 7946671 Trooper John Frederick Thorogood, who is buried in Uden Commonwealth War Cemetery. He explained that as a schoolboy of eleven years of age he had witnessed many aspects of the war but he had never forgotten the allied soldiers and airmen who had fought to liberate his country. It is his hobby to contact relatives of men who had died in battle in the vicinity of his town and to try to do something to perpetuate their memory.

   He was writing to me about my brother and I was able to provide him with a great deal of information which I had discovered concerning his death. Since that date my correspondence with Ad Hermens and several other Dutch people, who have been drawn into the story in consequence of his enquiries, has become quite extensive and revealing. Events have ensued which I now feel it worthy to relate both in memory of my mother and my brother John and all those men of the 44th Royal Tank Regiment who gave their lives in defence of their country. I also wanted to write this as a tribute to my Dutch friends, both old and new, who have over many years unfailingly shown me and my family kindness and hospitality beyond our expectations – an attribute which seems to be widespread in that land towards allied veterans and their families.

I would like to dedicate this book to many people, whose names are mentioned in this book, and to the following people in particular:

The family Van Uden of St Oedenrode

Jan and Stine Heesen of Uden

Ad and Pia Hermans of Geldrop, without whose interest and research this book would never have been written

Henri van Weert of St Oedenrode, whose several contributions have assisted with this narrative

Toon, Anneke, Dorus and Mien van Weert of St Oedenrode

Toos and Ties Verstegen of Uden

Louis and Jeanny Kleijne of St Oedenrode

The Schepens family, in whose garden in de Ollandseweg, opposite Rijsingen, the memorial plinth is situated

Thanks are due to members of my family and friends who gave encouragement, but especially to Moayad who gave me considerable practical assistance in producing the final draft.

A very special mention to Samantha Larmour, my daughter Gillian's godchild, whose endeavours and hard work led to the publication of this book.

Those gallant warriors of the 44th who 'did their bit' for Britain and survived. To the likes of them we should be forever indebted.

Introduction

ALL TOO OFTEN DURING WARS WHEN THE DEATH OF A SON WAS NOTIFIED, many a mother could not bring herself to believe that her loved one was dead. During World War II the author's mother, sixty four year old widow Mary Ann Thorogood, was informed that her second son, John, had been killed in action in north west Europe on September 21st 1944 whilst serving as a tank gunner with 'C' Squadron of the 44th Royal Tank Regiment.

At the time she was living alone in Handsworth, Birmingham, with both sons serving abroad; the elder, George, being in India. She had to bear this tragic loss alone and had great difficulties coming to terms with it, living in the hope that her much loved son John would return some day. George, upon his repatriation from India in December 1944, promised that he would try to lay the ghost by proving to his mother that John had died in action. This is the story of how he did this and of the generous help and friendship he received – and continues to receive – from many Dutch people

Duty Calls

SEPTEMBER 3RD 1939, THAT FATEFUL DAY WHEN THE PRIME MINISTER OF Great Britain announced to the nation that Britain was again at war with Germany, was to herald a change in the lives of millions of people throughout the world. This story is how it affected our small family – my fifty nine year old mother, my brother John, aged sixteen, and myself, aged twenty.

My mother was recovering from what must have been a very traumatic period in her life. Having been a regular soldier in the 11th and later the 13th Hussars my father had been disabled in World War I and was discharged as medically unfit for further service on October 16th 1919. After his discharge he had frequent bouts of illness and declining health eventually necessitated his giving up work in 1927. My mother then nursed him until he died in January 1930.

Mother was left with three young children to support, together with an ageing aunt, Emma, who had cared for her since the death of her mother when she was a child of four. With no army pension she had to manage on her depleted savings supplemented by a widow's pension and allowances for each of her children that amounted to an approximate total of eighty five pence per week in today's currency. In 1933 both Aunt Emma and my seventeen year old sister, Mary Louisa, died. It was a very difficult time for mother and to make ends meet she occasionally sold or pawned a piece of jewellery.

By 1939 our financial position was improving, albeit slowly, for both John and I were in work and contributing to the family finances. Mother devoted herself exclusively to us boys, for no other man ever featured in her life after father's death. We were a very happy trio and devoted to each other. The announcement by Chamberlain was a silent and unforgettable moment for all of us, but particularly so for mother. She had already suffered, as had many millions of women of her generation, from the tragedies of the previous war; her married life had been marred by father's illness and she had known the fear and dread of losing a loved one in battle. Now, after a short period of twenty years, in the autumn of her life, she had to face the prospect of her sons having to go to war. All that she had striven for – a safe and comfortable haven for herself and her boys – was likely to be shattered in the forthcoming conflict.

I had already by that time registered for National Service. Within a few weeks of the outbreak of war I received instructions to report to Norton Barracks, Worcester, where I was to be trained as an infantryman in the Worcestershire Regiment. Mother had always instilled into us duty both to our family and to our country. The first thing she did after war was declared was to enrol, with John, into the Air Raid Precautions' service (ARP). They were stationed at Kent Street Baths in Birmingham as voluntary unpaid nursing auxiliaries.

I reported to Norton Barracks on October 16th 1939, twenty years to the day that my father had been discharged after World War I. My basic training at Worcester lasted for three months and early in 1940 I was given seven days embarkation leave. This was spent at home in Benacre Street with mother and John, at the end of which I took leave of my many friends. I vividly recall looking around the living room of our home and of going upstairs to the bedroom I shared with John for a final look at those familiar surroundings before setting off on the start of my long journey to India. My father had been stationed with the 13th Hussars at Meerut when the war broke out in 1914. By mid December 1914 that regiment had landed in France as part of the Meerut Cavalry Brigade and were soon in the trenches before Festubert in an infantry role.

The Worcestershire Regiment had two battalions, both serving abroad. The 1st battalion was in North Africa and the 2nd battalion was on active service on the North West Frontier of India. The 2nd Worcesters had gained immortal fame at the outset of World War I when the battalion, under the command of Major E B Hankey with twelve officers and 350 men, repulsed a German attack at Gheluvult which threatened to breach the British line. This effort on their part was called for by High Command after all other attempts to hold the line had failed. They not only drove the Germans back, but inflicted heavy casualties on the Bavarians and Saxons who opposed them. It is said that their action that day saved the line from complete collapse and staved off a possible German victory. On that crucial day, October 31st 1914, the battalion lost three officers and 184 men.

My departure from home was a sombre moment. Mother and John came to see me off at New Street station. There were no tears but as the train slowly pulled out I was glad that the darkness of the tunnel concealed my emotions, for some inner sense told me I should not see John again. Neither was I to see my home, for that was destroyed in the bombing of Birmingham in November 1940.

On arrival in India on February 12th 1940 our draft of thirty men proceeded to Sialkot in the Punjab where the Depot of the 2nd Worcesters was situated. After a few days for acclimatization and kitting out for active service most of our draft were sent to join the battalion at Bannu on the North West Frontier. So, while I soldiered in the relative peace of India, mother and John began to shape their lives within the restrictions brought about by the intensification of war.

Mother received no financial support from the State for losing the income of a wage earner. Like many of my generation, on joining the services one was obliged to make a voluntary contribution to any dependent relative of seven shillings from a meagre pay of fourteen shillings (thirty five and seventy pence respectively in today's money). This one did quite willingly, but it left one very short of money, for the cost of cleaning materials and any regimental stoppages had to be met from the remaining money. Imagine today having to go to war for thirty five pence per week; that is how it was for those in the ranks.

On the night of October 26th 1940 a heavy raid by German aircraft left a trail of destruction across the City of Birmingham. Kent Street Baths, where both mother and John were on duty, was twice hit by incendiaries and high explosive bombs. Three people were killed and many injured, some of whom continued to work in spite of their wounds. While mother helped with the casualties, John (then seventeen) was fighting the fires caused by the incendiaries and trying to keep the flames in check. It was reported in the Birmingham Evening Mail that John and our mutual friend twenty year old Sydney Broadfield – who were both unpaid volunteers – worked with the Chief Baths Attendant Mr George Dolphin for ninety minutes to contain the blaze until the fire service arrived. John was commended for his conspicuous bravery on that night by the Earl of Dudley, the Regional Commissioner for ARP in Birmingham.

As the war progressed air raids became more frequent in

Birmingham and many other major cities in the United Kingdom. Mother and John continued to do their nightly duties at Kent Street, despite John having to work in the daytime. Then one November night after another heavy raid they found that their own home had also been bombed and was now uninhabitable. They had to salvage what they could from the debris and look for temporary accommodation elsewhere. No help was available from the City Council, who were undoubtedly having great difficulty in housing the homeless, so Mother and John found temporary refuge in Handsworth with mother's cousins George and Doris Harrison. After some months they moved to live with mother's aunt in Newcombe Road, but eventually they found a flat for themselves in nearby Antrobus Road. Meanwhile they had transferred their ARP duties to Grove Lane Baths, where mother continued to serve until the end of the war and John until he was called up in January 1942.

John registered for National Service in the summer of 1941 and was called up into the Royal Armoured Corps in January 1942. He had tried to enlist earlier, when aged seventeen, but was forestalled by mother who declared his true age. On January 15th 1942, he left home to join Troop 126 'D' Squadron 61st Training Regiment, Assay Barracks, at Tidworth. After a period of field and battle training he was transferred to 'C' Squadron, 52nd Training Regiment, at Bovington Camp, Dorset.

On completion of his training as a soldier in the Royal Armoured Corps John was given embarkation leave from June 22nd to July 7th 1942 which he spent at home with mother. Shortly after returning to Bovington he proceeded overseas en route to the Middle East, although mother had no idea to which part of the world he was heading. The convoy of troopships docked at the port of Cape Town, South Africa, where allied soldiers always received generous hospitality from the local populace. John recorded in his diary that he was befriended by a Cape Dutch family and went out with a Dutch nurse called Elsabe Dannyk of the Rondesbosh Cottage Hospital, Rosebank, Capetown. A ticket found in a wallet suggests that they went up Table Mountain for their first date. One of John's letters revealed that a second date was arranged, but unfortunately he missed the appointment – they were recalled early to their ship and he sailed without being able to contact her. In 1990 I tried to contact this lady but without success; the newspapers to whom I wrote failed to respond to my letters.

John arrived in the Middle East in September 1942. After initial posting to No. 1 Squadron Middle East RAC School and Base Depot, he was sent to join 'B' Squadron of the 41st Royal Tank Regiment. His twentieth birthday was celebrated in Alexandria. On December 18th 1942 he was posted as one of 156 reinforcement to the depleted 44th Royal Tank Regiment, where he joined 'C' Squadron, with which he was to remain throughout his service. The regiment was then located at Rafah where it was reforming after being continuously in action in North Africa since 1941.

This Regiment was formed in 1938 from the Territorial Battalion of the 6th Glosters (an Infantry Regiment) into an armoured unit. The 44th were mobilised on September 3rd 1939, immediately on the outbreak of war, and were on active service in the United Kingdom until April 1941, when they sailed for the Middle East in the troopship, *SS Sobieski*. On arrival in Egypt, initially for a month, the Regiment formed part of the 4th Armoured Brigade, but then took its place with the 8th RTR and the 42nd RTR to form the 1st Army Tank Brigade.

Equipped with Matilda tanks, the Regiment was actively engaged in desert operations against German and Italian forces, their first battle being operation 'Crusader' in November 1941, the relief of Tobruk, Sidi Omar and Omar Nuova, Gazala, and the defence of the 150 Brigade Box. The latter was a desperate and hard fought battle which resulted in very heavy losses in both men and tanks.

At Rafah they began training on the new Grant tanks, forerunner of the Shermans. Shortly after joining the Regiment John wrote home to mother to say he was very happy with his new unit and had settled in quite well. His other news was that on New Year's Eve he went to the local races where he won five shillings. This was almost a week's pay, after the deduction of his voluntary allowance to mother.

In April 1943 John went on a week's leave to Tel Aviv, Jerusalem and Bethlehem, visiting all the holy places. On his return the Regiment began combined training operations at Kabrit, on completion of which they moved to Amaniya near Alexandria where their Grant tanks were replaced with the new Shermans. On June 23rd 1943 the 44th moved to Suez where it was fully re-equipped, trained and made ready for battle again.

'Headquarters', 'B' and 'C' Squadrons embarked at Suez on *HTS Orontees* from where they sailed for the Mediterranean Sea via Port Said and joined the vast convoy of ships heading for the invasion of Sicily where the 44th RTR was to form part of the 4th Armoured Brigade in the 50th Northumbrian Division. The 44th was to remain with the 4th Armoured Brigade until the end of the war in Europe.

The invasion of Sicily took place on July 10th 1943 and the Regiment was again involved in many bloody engagements against a determined enemy. One fierce action was the attack on Primosole Bridge, which was stoutly defended by parachutists of the Herman Goring Parachute Brigade. This was followed by the advance on Catania and Messina, the taking of which brought an end to the Sicilian campaign with the defeat of the Axis forces. The 44th concentrated south of Paterno where the squadrons rested, re-equipped and engaged in training and range firing in preparation for their future involvement in the Italian campaign.

It may seem unfair to select for special mention one particular action from among many in which the Regiment had been involved, having regard to the unusually high number of decorations awarded to officers and men, several of whom were decorated twice for their gallantry. However, an action that took place in the early stages of the Sicily campaign is worthy of mention. In this the sheer amount of enemy guns and vehicles destroyed, and general officers captured, was unusual by any standards and serves as an example of the fighting spirit of the men in the regiment. This was the brilliant engagement fought on July 13th, three days after landing, by Sergeant Hampson, Commanding No. 5 Troop of 'C' Squadron, and ably assisted by a Sergeant Boyce and Corporal Frank Lea.

They attacked an enemy column and destroyed five enemy tanks, an ammunition lorry, four staff cars and several more lorries and motor cycles. As the road was blocked with all the resulting debris of the battle, Sergeant Hampson, in the face of machine gun fire and assisted by Corporal Lea, dismounted from their tanks and went forward on foot to capture a divisional General, his three Staff Brigadiers and five Staff Officers. The troop then continued to advance against the enemy and later disposed of three tanks, three 105mm guns and twenty nine more trucks and motor cycles, besides taking many prisoners. All three NCO's were decorated for their bravery on that day.

In late September the Regiment landed at Taranto in Italy from where they moved on Manfredonia. They were again soon in action in the area of Serracapriola, Sangro River, San Salvo, Vasto, Capello, Monte Rocca, Paglieta, San Vito, Mooro River and Rualti, this last engagement being in support of the Princess Patricia's Light Infantry of Canada. The 44th fought its last battle in Italy at Treglia where orders were received to return to the United Kingdom to bolster the forthcoming invasion of Europe with seasoned and battle-hardened troops.

They embarked on the troopship *Ranchi* and reached home shores on February 8th 1944. Back in England they were once again stationed in the seaside town of Worthing on the south coast and, having been resident in that place before departing for Egypt in 1942, they were welcomed back by the local population as old friends.

John's return to England was an unexpected surprise to mother. She recorded her emotions in her diary:

> Red Letter Day – John is in England. How excited I am, can't do anything right, feel all topsy turvey with excitement. From 12th February until 6th March, all one glorious time with John. Now he has gone back again to Worthing how I miss him.

After the period of disembarkation leave, enjoyed no doubt by all members, the Regiment journeyed to Scotland for exercises in range firing, adapting to the new Sherman tank fitted with the seventeen pounder gun known as the 'Firefly'. These were allocated on the basis of one to each troop of 75mm Shermans.

For the few months of his stay in Worthing John was befriended by a family living in Mansfield Close, with whom he spent much of his free time. They were very good to him and mother made several visits to them after the war.

Mother's entire married life, which did not begin until 1916 when she married father at the mature age of thirty five, was marred by war. The help she received from official sources was negligible, yet she seldom complained. People in those days were proud and independent and the Welfare State had not arrived to erode those characteristics such as honesty, pride, thrift and self reliance which were the hallmark of much of pre-war society. The Government's parsimonious treatment of the disabled, the widows and dependants was a disgrace, with any assistance beyond the very minimal benefits which they reluctantly doled out having to be 'topped' by such worthy charitable organisations as the British Legion and the Soldiers, Sailors and Airmens Association. Things have now improved somewhat, but assistance given during and following the two world wars was deplorable for those many thousands who had suffered grievous loss – for the most part they were abandoned and ignored by the powers that be. My mother was one such person but for all the tragedies which beset her she always showed a determination to master her difficulties, to be independent and self reliant. She was beautiful, loving, kind and generous and devoted to her family – a woman without peer and I loved her for all those endearing qualities.

A One Way Journey

It was the eve of D Day. Training had finished. The Regiment was as well prepared for battle as it could possibly be to face the forthcoming conflict in Europe. The day of departure had arrived, when the Regiment had once more to take its leave of the good people of Worthing. It was to the accompanying tears and cheers of their Worthing friends that engines were started up, the last waves of farewell given, and the Regiment began to move. Bristling with all the armour of war it left the town to join the huge convoys of vehicles that were converging onto the Portsmouth Road, heading for the ports where they were to embark with the vast armada of ships which formed the largest invasion fleet of all time. Well over six thousand ships had been assembled to convey the invading army which was to attack the coast of Normandy to liberate Europe from under the heel of the jackboot. As they set off to do battle once again with their old implacable enemy, every man no doubt wondered whether his luck would hold in this final phase of the bitter and hard fought crusade to put an end to the evil of Nazism. For many their luck ran out.

Undoubtedly many of those war weary warriors – a high proportion of whom had been in action against the Axis forces in North Africa, Sicily and Italy continuously since 1941 – felt that they had already made their contribution to the war effort and were 'browned off' at being thrown once more into the fray so soon after returning to England. On July 28th John wrote to me:

> Well, the 8th (Army) has done a very great deal in this war, but I for one wish to forget it all once it is over; it will be like a bad dream to me, all of it. I only hope this war is over by the time you do come home George so that I shall have a very good chance of being there with you.

Due to bad weather the main body of the Regiment was delayed in their departure from Gosport by two days and did not reach Normandy until June 8th, two days later than planned. After disembarking the Regiment concentrated in the village of Amblie, near Cruelly, as part of the 4th Armoured Brigade, to act in a supporting role in the event of the Germans launching an armoured counter attack against the assault forces. But such an attack did not happen. On June 25th the 44th joined with the 11th Armoured Division in a concerted drive over the river Odon with the intention of securing and cutting off the high ground beyond the city of Caen. During the ensuing days, many bloody engagements between British and German armour took place; the 44th fighting in the vicinity of the village of Cheux, which was occupied. On June 29th the Regiment was involved in the fiercest battle yet. It repulsed a determined German counter attack and held open the Odon bridgehead, several other engagements being in the vicinity of hills 112, 113 and the villages of Gavrus, Evrecy and Esquay. Very heavy losses were sustained on both sides. The 44th lost thirteen tanks destroyed with three more damaged; nine men were killed, twenty seven wounded and nine missing. At the close of the action the

Regiment was switched to rejoin the 4th Armoured Brigade which expected a heavy enemy counter attack North of the Odon.

On July 10th the Regiment moved to the high ground opposite hill 112 in an infantry support role with the 43rd Wessex Division, in which my brother-in-law Douglas Woodward was serving with the 4th Dorsets. The 44th remained in the area, fully deployed in an anti-tank and counter attack role until the evening of July 18th. Throughout those eight days they were constantly under heavy shell fire, mortaring and strafing from the air by the opposing German forces. This constant bombardment confined crews to their tanks which resulted in loss of both sleep and food. With brief rest intervals, but always at the ready to engage a desperate enemy, the Regiment then came under the command of the 3rd British Division during the period of August 5th – 10th and in direct support of the 9th Infantry Brigade, whose allotted task was to cut the main Vire-Caen Road. Each Squadron of the Regiment was allocated to support an Infantry battalion. The subsequent fighting took place in the bocage country which was composed of small fields, high hedges and banks, interspersed with woods. This type of country provided ideal concealment and camouflage to the benefit of the defending Germans who fought desperately to hold every inch of ground. The bocage country cost the attacking British forces many casualties, particularly from snipers.

By mid August the concerted attacks by the Americans, British and Canadian forces resulted in the German 7th Army Group being surrounded on all sides. Their only route of escape from annihilation was in the area of the town of Falaise. The role of the 4th Armoured Brigade, in concert with the 53rd Welsh Division, was to put the squeeze on the neck of the Falaise pocket with the object of preventing the German forces escaping. After several difficulties arising from the type of terrain the Regiment had to cross, which necessitated the use of hedge cutter tanks to carve a way through the high banks and hedges, they reached their positions. There a most unpleasant night was spent due to mortaring and constant rain.

Early in the morning of August 18th the Regiment was ordered to take up forward positions on the high ground overlooking the Falaise-Argetan road. To quote from *A History of the 44th Royal Tank Regiment*:

> Meantime the rest of the Regiment had formed up on the side of the hill overlooking the valley and the last road for the Boche. As it got lighter, the floor of the valley was seen to be alive with movement – men marching, cycling and running, columns of horse-drawn transport, motor transport, and as the sun got up, even more and more targets. Soon the whole Regiment was banging away with all it had, the cry for more ammunition went up on all sides, and the echelon was kept fully occupied. It was a gunner's paradise and everybody took advantage of it.
>
> It was a quite unbelievable sight and one which will never be repeated. Away on our left was the famous killing ground, and all day the roar of Typhoons went on and fresh columns of smoke obscured the horizon. From our position we could just see one short section of the Argentan-Trun road, some two hundred yards in all, on which sector at one time was crowded the whole miniature picture of an army in rout. First a squad of men running, being overtaken by men on bicycles followed by a limber at a gallop, and the whole being overtaken by a Panther tank crowded with men and doing well up to 30mph, all with the main idea of getting away as fast as they could. The Germans will never again be able to say that their army was not defeated.
>
> That evening our infantry division came up and we pulled back to a leaguer in the middle of the Corps gun area. It poured with rain all the night and the next morning, so an enjoyable time was had by all.

However, at 1700 hours on 21st August the Regiment was called forward and told to go into the middle of the killing ground and ensure that all the enemy there had been liquidated. This was brought about by the attempt that had been made by the Germans to break out the night before. We were told to contact the Canadians on the line Falaise-Trun and the Americans on the line Argentan-Trun. And so into the middle we went in the pouring rain. During the night Guepres, Valledieu les Bailleul, and Tournai-sur-Dives were occupied, the main obstacle to movement being the wreckage, as all the roads and lanes were choked with vehicles, carts, dead horses and men. Prisoners were also a source of embarrassment, thousands of them wandering about waiting to give themselves up to somebody. We alone collected over three thousand, together with innumerable tanks, guns and vehicles.

In spite of Brigade Headquarters having sent out liaison officers to all the surrounding formations and nationalities we were shelled good and heavy from all sides, luckily with not much damage to us. Dawn broke and we moved forward to the last lap, occupied Aubry-en-Exmimes and contacted the Americans at Chambois and the Canadians at Magny. The Major in charge there had won the VC the night before, though he didn't know it and couldn't have cared less, as sleep was his aim and object at the time. However, he tore his gunner off a pretty strip for shooting us up.

The villagers soon came to life and we were pelted with flowers and calvados, and later in the day, when the sun came up, by requests to move the dead horses. The village of Tournai had four hundred, so the Burgomaster proudly informed us, and would we do something about it. We didn't, as we had enough of our own.

So ended the Falaise battle and the German 7th Army Group, and we sat back in a de-horsed orchard and prepared for the 'swan' through France.

John wrote again to me on August 11th:

> When I am sitting down by myself I often wonder what it will be like seeing you again George, how much you have altered, but from your letters pal you are the same old brother of mine. The war is well on the way to its end now, isn't it? And a good job too for I am getting very sick of it. Jerry seems in a bad state out here but I don't go too much by that as I know what he is. He is certainly not super human as some people seem to think. He's just as liable to get lead poisoning as anyone else.

Advancing on August 23rd to cross the river Seine the Regiment encountered no opposition, but progress was delayed due to the mass of wreckage and dead horses which barred all forward routes in the area. Crossing the Seine on August 26th and advancing on a wide front across country the Regiment entered Gourney-en-Bray on August 30th where the local populace gave them a great welcome. Pushing on, 'C' Squadron fought a short but sharp action and knocked out three anti-tank guns while 'B' Squadron was engaged in a similar action at Grand Villiers. The Regiment occupied Poix by nightfall on August 31st, having destroyed in their advance a long enemy column of horse-drawn transport. Over eight hundred prisoners were taken at Poix and a vast amount of equipment destroyed. Again they received a great but brief welcome from the local citizens, for by the next morning the 44th were headed towards the river Somme. The Somme, that bloodied ground of World War I, scene of the loss of thousands of allied soldiers; where on that fateful day – July 1st 1916 – the British Army alone suffered sixty thousand casualties before lunch.

Due to all bridges in the vicinity of the advance having been blown by the retreating Germans, the 44th were directed to advance via the northern outskirts of Amiens in the area of Berneuil. They motored all night in the brilliant moonlight and encountered no enemy opposition. By the time it went into leaguer the next morning the Regiment had covered 100 miles. Working in support of the 7th Armoured Division, the task for the Regiment on September 2nd was to clear and open up routes for the 7th Division to pass through to take the town of Ghent. 'A' Squadron successfully attacked Berneuil, destroying in the process enemy transport of the 859 Grenadier Regiment and capturing many prisoners, thus allowing the 7th Division to pass through. On September 5th, the Regiment rejoined the 7th Division in the area of Ghent and leaguered that night near Helchin.

Moving again on September 6th, with 'B' Squadron in the lead, the Regiment crossed into Belgium meeting opposition at the village of Wortegem where a battery of six German 105mm field guns opposed their advance. These, however, were quickly overrun and with 'B' Squadron remaining in the Wortegem area to mop up, the Regiment deployed 'A' and 'C' Squadrons in the area of Anseghem. There, from high ground positions, they were able to inflict much damage against enemy columns seen to be moving along the lower ground.

At the nearby village of Avelghem a fierce battle followed and several tanks were destroyed. There followed what must be regarded as the most confusing battle ever fought by the 44th RTR. To quote from the historical record:-

> Trouble commenced with 'A' Squadron on the left. Lieut. Ottino, whose tank had broken a track, remained behind with the other tanks of his troop, fortunately just off the main road, when he heard sounds of movement on the road. Going to have a look, he saw a large mixed column of enemy vehicles on the move down the road, almost following on the heels of 'A' Squadron. Meantime the rest of 'A' Squadron were quite happily withdrawing further to the east, led by Capt. Joe Rogers, Major Dick Cave being at Regimental Headquarters

getting orders for the night. Coming on to the main road from the track down which they were moving Capt. Rogers' tank collided with an enemy half-track. His and Ottino's reports came in almost simultaneously and there was no doubt that a very large German force was involved. The Commanding Officer ordered Ottino to continue mending his track and to go into hiding where he was. Rogers and his 'A' Squadron party were told to switch off and let the enemy move on where they would run slap into 'C' Squadron, and to 'recce' ways out and to guard against being surprised. By now it was quite dark and for the second time in the Regimental story Joe Rogers and the Commanding Officer were carrying out whispered conversations on the 19 set, with the enemy only a few yards away from Joe! 'B' Squadron meantime moved in behind 'C', not without a certain amount of adventure and a few turns left instead of right.

Major Dick Cave, 'A' Squadron Commander, mustering two tanks on the right side of the enemy, moved up and joined 'C' Squadron and he and Major Teddy Foster organised a hedgehog of tank troops covering all approaches. Meanwhile Joe Rogers had brought his infantry platoon forward and had dismounted some Browning guns. Then fell an uneasy silence which lasted till 2350 hours. Then all hell broke loose and continued for the rest of the night.

The first event was the 'brewing up' of Joe Rogers' two leading tanks, apparently by gunfire at point-blank range. Lieut. Baker, who was in the third tank in line, was wounded, but was joined by Lieut. Osborne, who took command and led the two tanks of the troop straight forward at the enemy on the main road, followed by the next troop commanded by Lieut. Hooper. The flames from the burning tanks now lit up the scene as the two troops headed for the rest of 'A' and 'C' Squadron positions. The place was alive with enemy infantry and vehicles who were now caught in the cross-fire from the two parties. Great carnage was done and seventeen enemy vehicles and over fifty dead were seen the next morning. In the confusion Lieut. Hooper's tank ran off the road into a ditch, crushing several of the enemy en route. Four tanks got through to the 'C' Squadron position and withdrew to Kerkhoven to reorganise. Capt. Joe Rogers and the rest of the 'A' Squadron had withdrawn northwards together with their element of the Recce Troop and platoon of the 2/60th and leaguered up for the night together with over fifty prisoners.

Despite this setback the enemy still continued to press eastwards by all roads and tracks, but no longer in the direction of Kerkhoven and the bridge over the river, so our object had been achieved.

Intermittent action continued for the rest of the night, enemy self-propelled guns being particularly active. Major Dick Cave's tank was knocked out and his other disabled. Several echelon vehicles which were trying to replenish 'C' Squadron were also hit, and one of 'C' Squadron's tanks which was being worked on was brewed up, resulting in three killed and three wounded. 'B' Squadron also were shelled fairly heavily and that great old soldier of the Regiment, Sergeant Major Lobb, MM and bar, was killed by a direct hit. With the arrival of better shooting light we succeeded in putting paid to the self-propelled guns and a reasonable degree of quiet prevailed. A total of six officers and twenty-five German other ranks were captured during the engagement.

We were able to replenish and reorganise ourselves preparatory to setting out to rescue our cut-off elements. At about noon 46 Brigade of 15th Scottish Division arrived in Kerkhoven and a plot was laid on to attack the high ground to the north, thus clearing the main axis and possibly allowing Rogers and Ottino to break out.

The attack went in at 1500 hours led by 'B' Squadron. All went well, except that the infantry could not capture the village of Tieghem. However, 'A' and 'C' Squadrons fired high explosive into the village to keep the Germans' heads down. At 1530 hours Captain Rogers' party of two Shermans and one Stuart, carrying the platoon of 2/60th on their backs, broke cover and arrived back with us safely. They had had to abandon their fifty prisoners. At 1600 hours Ottino broke out and driving through scores of flabbergasted Germans he almost made it.

But just before he was home and dry his Troop Sergeant's tank, commanded by Sergeant Smythe, was knocked out. Smythe got back to us that night, complete with two prisoners he captured on the way, and the rest got back the next morning. We then withdrew with our infantry and whilst so doing Lieut. Osborne, MM, was fatally wounded by a stray bullet – a great loss.

That night we remained deployed with our infantry to prevent any further infiltration by the enemy, and passed a relatively peaceful night. Prisoner interrogation had revealed that the 712th German Infantry Division had been the cause of our troubles. They had been ordered to break out at midnight on 6th September. Their axis Ingoyghem-Tieghem-Kerkhoven passed straight through our position. To achieve this they had assembled all their anti-tank guns and artillery plus their mechanical transport at the head of the division with the intention of blasting a way through, so that the footsloggers and horse transport could follow. We had stopped them.

Among the injured was Captain Joe Rogers, who was evacuated to the United Kingdom and did not return to the Regiment until towards the end of hostilities.

On September 8th the Regiment leaguered in the area of Termonde and on the following day, as part of the 7th Armoured Division, were ordered to take the town of St Nicholas beyond the river Scheldt. By using a low classified wooden bridge and going across one tank at a time they entered the town at 11.30am. There an overjoyed population turned out in their thousands to welcome them and within minutes the Commanding Officer, Lieutenant Colonel G Hopkinson, was carried forward onto the steps of the Town Hall and given the freedom of the town. Tremendous crowds had gathered and these impeded the taking up of defensive positions; these had only just been established when a German Mark IV tank approached a position held by 'B' Squadron. Only with the

Above: My father (the Corporal) with his two brothers, my mother and uncle Grant Staples – a reunion photograph of three orphaned brothers who met up in 1916

Above: John, with mother, as a baby

Left: John, aged two or three

Left: John and mother in the garden at Antrobus Road, taken whilst he was in training and shortly before he went to Africa

Below left: John and mother at Earls Common, around 1941

Below: John with comrades in North Africa, late 1942

Above: John, aged 19

Above: Stanley Matthews

Left: John and Stan, probably taken in Belgium between 9th and 12th September 1944, shortly before both were killed

Above: The Market Place, St Oedenrode, where I began my search in November 1945

Above: Eerschot, where I first met Ben van Uden on November 24th 1945

Left: Ben van Uden

Above: Toni van Hommel

Above: Anna van Uden, the tireless worker

Above: The destroyed 'Firefly'

Above: De Ollandeweg today. The tank was first hit opposite the house on the right. Seconds later it was hit again and careered on out of control until it was stopped by a tree opposite the second house. John was found in front of the house in the foreground and he and Stan were buried in the nearby field until June 12th 1946

Above: Mother at John's graveside in 1961

Above: Mother's last photograph – for her passport to The Netherlands

Left: John's grave, taken in 1994

Left: The church clock tower overlooking the military cemetery in Uden, which features in my poem at the front of this book

Below: My wife, Ivy, and I with our very good friends Jan and Stine Heesen and Ties Verstegen in 1991

greatest difficulty was the crowd moved out of the line of fire of the 'B' Squadron guard tank so that it could deal with the intruder, which it did to the thunderous applause of the crowd even though all the neighbouring windows of the shops were shattered. The Regiment remained in St Nicholas until midday September 12th and a great time was had by all in the liberated city. It was here, I believe, that the last photograph was taken of John and Stanley Matthews, surrounded by some of the local ladies and children, standing smiling in front of their 'Firefly'.

The 44th had possibly had more than their fair share of action during the 'swan' through France and Belgium. Unlike Normandy – where great devastation with bombardment from land, sea and air had been inflicted on almost every village and town – north of the Seine there was little damage caused, for the retreating Germans had moved fast and the advancing British met with limited opposition. Consequently, local populations were jubilant and ecstatic crowds greeted their liberators with great enthusiasm. Kisses were showered upon them, flowers bedecked their vehicles, wine and fruit was given in abundance and tears of joy flowed freely. Those who took part in those joyous occasions (I was not one of them) and who survived the war will never forget those unparalleled euphoric days. Hopefully, such scenes will never be repeated, for that type of war is now part of history. What that allied army did in the summer of 1944 was to herald the demise of dictators like Hitler, for that crusade revealed to the whole world that the ravaging and conquest of other lands was no longer an option.

John wrote to Mother on September 13th:

> I cannot remember whether I told you or not, mum, but the people are giving us a great reception out here. Fruit, beer, cigars and Lord knows what. I have been sleeping in civvy beds, having baths in people's homes. I met one very nice girl one day. Now don't get thinking I'm

losing my heart over a Belgian girl, but she was lovely. I had some fun with her. She could speak neither French nor English, and I could not speak Flemish, but we got on alright together. I said I had fell for her and was coming back to marry her – only joking of course. She went to some chaps who spoke English and asked what I had said. She came back, put her arms around my neck and was kissing me in front of about two hundred people. It's a good job I wasn't staying there for long or I might have been a married man now.

What was so remarkable was that the seemingly invincible German Army who, with their new 'Blitzkrieg' tactics in 1940 had trounced the small British Expeditionary Force sent to the aid of France and Belgium and, subsequently, came near to conquering the whole of Europe and Russia, was now being thrashed or, as Monty put it, 'knocked for six'. For the most part the allied armies, American, British and Canadian, with smaller patriot groups of French, Belgian and Dutch services were comprised of young men of nineteen to twenty three years of age with no previous battle experience. Supported by such blooded veteran formations as the 7th Armoured Division, 50th Northumbrian and 51st Highland Divisions – which were made up of regiments like the 44th RTR, who to their great credit had beaten the hun in North Africa, Sicily and Italy – they achieved one of the greatest victories in the history of warfare. They had destroyed the German army in France and Belgium as a fully effective fighting force and brought freedom to those countries which had suffered under Nazi domination for four long years. The Thousand Year Reich was about to crumble.

Following the rapid advances, rumour was rife that the war would soon be over. The exhilaration of liberation by the native population was shared by allied servicemen who began to believe they would soon be returning home to their families. On August 27th John wrote to me:

> The way things are going Jerry has just about had it anyway. Chaps are betting when it will be over, and some say in a fortnight's time. I wouldn't like to take a bet on it.

Despite the crushing defeats inflicted upon them, the Germans were not finished. In retreat they proved in the main to be as resolute as they were in attack. Determined to inflict as much damage as possible on the allied forces and refusing to concede ground without a fight, it took another eight months to bring them to heel. That was only achieved after their homeland had been completely overrun and their armies crushed between the converging allied forces; so after the 'swan' there was still much fighting to be done. To General Montgomery's bitter and lasting disappointment, particularly following the success of his strategy which resulted in the defeat of the German army in France, the overall command of the allied forces in North West Europe was assumed by General Eisenhower as from September 1st 1944. No doubt this was due to Monty's somewhat abrasive manner in his dealings with his American colleagues, among whom there was resentment at being under his direct command.

The revelries of the 44th in St Nicholas were short lived for they had been chosen to protect the line of advance of 30 corps in that ill fated operation known as 'Market Garden'. This was based on an idea conceived by the now Field Marshall Montgomery to seize the final river crossing over the Rhine at Arnhem. This would enable the allied forces, once over that river, to quickly encircle the Ruhr and cut Germany off from her vital industrial base which he firmly believed would cause the Germans to capitulate and thus bring the war to a speedy end. This conception was contrary to the strategy adopted by the Americans, who intended to conduct the war by advancing into Germany on a broad front. There was much controversy between the Field Marshall and his American colleagues, but eventually Monty got his way with the promise of US backing.

The airborne troops taking part were to be the American 101st and 82nd Airborne Divisions which would drop along a corridor route some sixty miles long stretching from the outskirts of the Dutch town of Eindhoven and onward to Nijmegen, securing all bridges en route. These bridges were: the Wilhelmena Canal at Son; the River Dommel at St Oedenrode; the Zuid Willemsvaart Canal at Veghel; the River Maas at Grave; the River Waal at Nijmegen. The 1st British Airborne Division, supported by the 1st Polish Parachute Brigade, were to drop in the area of Arnhem to secure the road bridge over the Neder Rhine, which was the final and most vital of all the bridges. With all the bridges in allied hands, it was conceived that the advancing armies could speedily pass through Dutch territory, cross over into Germany and quickly secure a base from which to attack and encircle the Ruhr, so vital to Germany's conduct of the War.

The role of the 44th RTR, under overall US command, was to act in concert with the US 101st Airborne Division to establish a series of piquets along 'The Corridor' to prevent the enemy attacking the vital line of march of the British 30 Corps, under the command of General Horrocks. With the British 12 and 8 Corps on the left and right flanks respectively they were to advance simulataneously. The central thrust by 30 Corps was to be led by the Guards Armoured Division, with the Irish Guards in the van. Their urgent task was to link up with the British 1st Airborne Division at Arnhem within the anticipated two, or at maximum three, days. After the successful and speedy 'swan' across France and Belgium this did not appear to be a difficult or impossible undertaking.

Apparently, when orders were received to proceed on the morning of September 17th, half of the Regiment were still hitting the high spots in the recently liberated town of Brussels and by the time all had rejoined many had not recovered from their exploits of the night before. The Regiment concentrated in the area north of the Hechtel crossroads and were joined, under 44th RTR command, by 'C' Squadron of the Royals, and 342 Battery of the 86th Field Regiment, RA. The narrow road along which they were to operate became known as 'The Corridor' and is still referred to as such by today's locals – the main road through the market place of St Oedenrode is named 'The Corridor' and a newspaper is published by that title in that town. On September 18th and 19th the Regiment stood by ready to move as the long columns of the Guards Armoured Division moved to their start positions. At 6pm on September 19th the move forward began and it was not long before contact was made with the enemy. And so the battle of the road began. While 'B' Squadron moved in the direction of Nuenen; 'C' Squadron, in concert with a squadron of 15/19th Hussars, proceeded along the main route and were soon engaged in a fierce armour-piercing battle, when they destroyed several self-propelled guns. 'B' Squadron, meanwhile, had destroyed two Mark IV tanks of the 107 Panzer Brigade in Opwetten but on reaching the town of Nuenen lost two of their own. Later in the day 'B' Squadron, with the support of 'A' Squadron, returned to the attack at Nuenen against the enemy and destroyed two more Mark IV's and several half-tracks. Meanwhile, 'C' Squadron advanced on St Oedenrode where it came under the command of 502 US Parachute Infantry Regiment. When it was established that the enemy were withdrawing the Regiment went into leaguer at Eindhoven.

At first light on September 21st the Regiment moved again to St Oedenrode where 'B' Squadron was ordered along 'The Corridor' route towards Veghel while 'C' Squadron, acting under the orders of Lieutenant Colonel Cassidy, Commanding 2nd Battalion of 502 Parachute Infantry Regiment, moved to the left

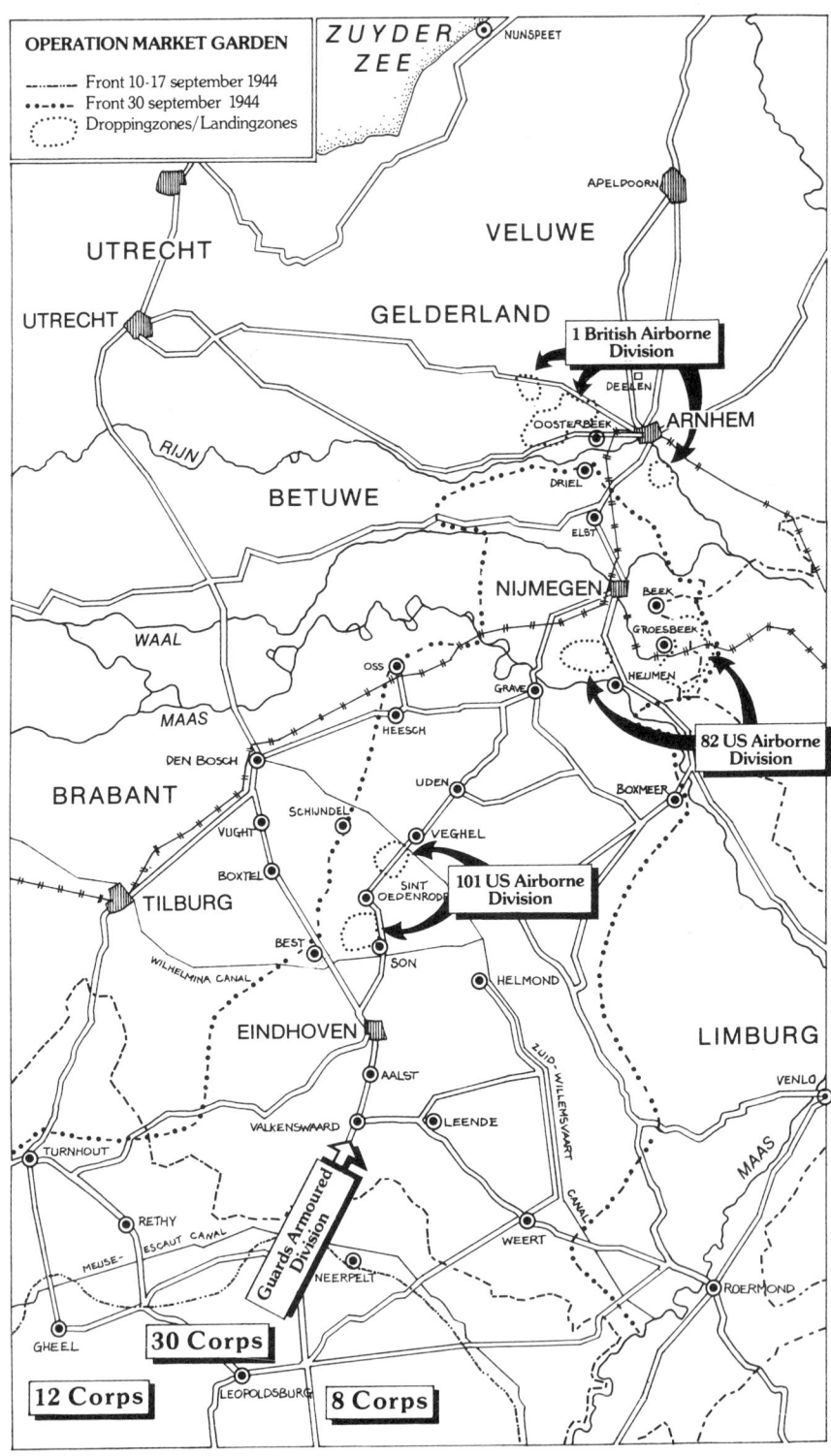

of 'The Corridor' – one troop along de Ollandseweg in the direction of Boxtel, the second troop in the direction of Schijndel. The object of both troops was to establish defensive positions on these vital routes to prevent the German forces from attacking and severing the main axis of 30 Corps advance.

Lieutenant David Cohen, commanding 4 Troop of 'C' Squadron, led the advance along de Ollandseweg. His tank was crewed by Trooper Stanley Matthews, the driver; Trooper 'Jack' Thorogood, the gunner; and a wireless operator whose name is unknown. As the tank was advancing along that road in the direction of the village of Olland, it was knocked out by German anti-tank fire and both Stanley Matthews and John were killed. Lieutenant Cohen sustained severe wounds as, I believe, did the wireless operator.

All that mother and I knew about the incident was the information sent in a very kind letter of condolence by Major E W Foster, DSO, MC, who had served continuously with the 44th RTR throughout the war, and had been in command of 'C' Squadron since late 1942. As his decorations show, he is a man of great courage. Jack, as John was known in the regiment, had at one time been Major Foster's gunner. His letter of September 23rd, repeated below, was couched in very personal and sympathetic terms and was a great comfort to mother, if ever such a letter can be:-

Dear Mrs Thorogood,

By now you will have received the official notification that your son, Jack, as he was known to us, has been killed in action.

This is then a very personal note to you from me because while you lose a son, I lose in Jack a battle comrade with whom I was long very closely associated. He was gunner on my own tank when we were abroad and having lived so closely with him I had grown not only to appreciate his efficiency and willing work but to value him as a friend, for his personal qualities. With Jack's sad death I find myself as the last surviving member of this old crew. I hope you may feel in these circumstances a little of your burden of loss is therefore shared by me, with you. All Jack's many friends here will also associate themselves with me in this sense.

Our job recently has been to defend the long route of the 2nd Army through the Netherlands. It has been a hard fought and bitter role, but we have succeeded. If the enemy had managed to cut across the road he would not only have had an exit for his own troops back into Germany but also he would have had at his mercy the unprotected supply units of our line of communication. Many hundreds of men would have been shot up. Truly those of our Officers and men who gave their lives in this battle gave their lives 'for their friends'.

Lieutenant Cohen was the Commander of the tank in which Jack was gunner. He was ordered to take his tanks up a road, down which the Germans were gradually pushing down towards the road axis. The troop successfully pushed back the enemy until suddenly two of the tanks were hit by enemy anti-tank weapons.

Mr Cohen was seen by the tank behind to be lifting Jack out of the tank after it was hit. About twenty seconds after the first hit, the tank was hit again and this shot killed poor Jack outright. Lieutenant Cohen was wounded and blown back on to the road.

I am happier to feel that there was no time for Jack to feel any pain. We can be certain of that. I hope that this letter will bring to you some little assistance in your loss. My own home address is Westbury Park, Bristol, 6, and I know my mother would be delighted to see you if you should be able to visit her there at any time. Perhaps later we may be able to meet ourselves. Meanwhile my mother may be able to give you more recent news of our activities.

Yours very sincerely and with deep sympathy,

E W Foster

The news of John's death reached me in India on October 6th 1944, almost simultaneously with the news that having completed almost five years abroad I was to be repatriated. At that time I was stationed in Thal Fort on the North West Frontier of what was then British India but since partition is now in Pakistan. I was serving with Thal Brigade and we were located about eight miles from the Afghan border at the southern end of the Kurram Valley, one of the vulnerable access routes into India from the north.

A colleague appeared with an envelope in his hand. Smiling, he gave it to me with the comment "Here it is, now you can start packing"; this remark being founded on the fact that I was expecting my repatriation orders for my return to the UK.

The shock I received when I read the message conveyed by the India Posts and Telegraph Department, stunned me. It read:

News from War Office – John killed Sept 21 – Mother Thorogood

I was utterly devastated, my thoughts immediately flying to mother in England who would at that moment be suffering alone the pangs of loss; mine were only just beginning. I immediately despatched to her a telegram of sympathy, assuring her that I would be home soon.

We had some nights previously been told by our signaller Sergeant, who had been listening to the radio traffic, of the fierce battle raging in the Netherlands, which turned out to be the 'Market Garden' operation. I did not, of course, know whether John was involved but I did know he had been actively engaged in the invasion of Normandy and expected he was still with the allied armies advancing rapidly across France.

During the following days my emotions were in turmoil. Outwardly I tried to show no weakness, but in the quiet of my quarters I don't mind admitting that my anguish and sorrow were fully released. I found it difficult to accept that my dear cheerful brother and friend, for whose safety I had always said a nightly prayer and who had so much to live for, was no more. My belief in prayer was shattered. Life would never be the same again without him. The fear which had haunted me ever since we parted in January 1940 had become a reality.

So it was in that bleak and inhospitable but relatively safe corner of the British Empire, whose earth held the remains of many soldiers of the Raj, and where fate had decreed I should serve my country, that I received this heartbreaking news.

Mother, John and I had been discussing in our letters the possibility of a reunion in the not too distant future, particularly having regard to the satisfactory progress of the war in Europe, where the allied armies were making rapid advances. But now my mind was full of what mother, at the age of sixty four, must be suffering.

She had shared so much with John during the early years of the war; the blitz of Birmingham, the loss of friends killed in the air raids, the destruction of their home, food shortages and the general discomforts of war. She had no brothers or sisters to whom she could turn for consolation and she was bearing her sorrow very much alone. It was with these thoughts in mind that two weeks after I received that fateful telegram, I departed from Thal on October 20th en route to the UK.

My ship sailed from Bombay in a huge convoy containing many thousands of time-expired men. We proceeded via Suez and the Mediterranean Sea where we were escorted by a 'Woolworth' type of aircraft carrier, a cruiser or two and several destroyers. The Mediterranean had recently reopened to general shipping and our passage through it was uneventful. We landed at Liverpool on December 8th 1944.

On reaching my home in Handsworth late on the evening of December 9th, instead of the mature homely figure I remembered from January 1940 there stood before me at the door a stooped, frail, grey haired old lady. I hardly recognised her, for her face was lined with grief for the loss of the son she had so much adored and who she could not bring herself to believe was dead. Nevertheless, she was a woman of great determination and spirit and my homecoming did much to help her recover to something like her old self. I had a full month's disembarkation leave and we spent this together, talking much about John. I tried many times to convince her that she must accept the inevitable, but she seemed unable to bring herself to believe she would never see him again. She had, as it were, closed her mind to that fact.

Throughout the war the only financial help she received was that allotted by John and myself. We contributed as much as our pay would allow and this was supplemented by a small salary she later received from her ARP work. On John's death she was awarded fifteen shillings per week as a pension but one year later this was withdrawn when she became eligible for the old age pension. At about the same time that she received the state retirement pension her work with the ARP came to an end. She therefore applied to the Army Paymaster for extra financial assistance but this was refused so she looked for another way to support herself.

Throughout the war John's employer, the Knight Optical Company of Windmill Street, for whom John had worked since leaving school at the age of fourteen, had sent five shillings weekly to mother for her to bank for John to provide him with a small nest egg for when he returned. Not very much, one might think, but five shillings was five shillings in those days and in any case it was a very generous gesture by a caring and good employer. Following John's death (he was the only employee not to survive the war) the management wrote to mother to say they would continue to send her the five shillings indefinitely.

Rather than accept this, she asked if they would give her a job. This they generously did and so, at the age of sixty five, she began work there learning her son's trade and skills on the factory floor. She had never before worked in such a situation but fortunately they proved to be most kind and considerate employers and she was moved to office duties when work in the factory became too hard for her. She remained with the Knight Optical Company – despite periods of absence through illness and when bad weather prevented her getting to work (a journey involving three buses) and during which they continued to pay her full wages – until her eightieth birthday. The Production Manager, Mr Smith, was most kind to her, as was his successor, Mr Eadon Allen who had been an officer in a Tank Regiment during the war. They had a common bond of sorts, for he too had been wounded while serving as a 'Tanky'. Working for that firm proved to be a great boon to mother. It gave her not only financial independence, but she was working among people who had known John since he had started as a lad in 1936 and with whom he was always a popular figure. She was very happy in that environment for it gave her a new lease of life.

To Lay the Ghost

IN SPITE OF THE OBVIOUS TRUTH CONTAINED IN MAJOR FOSTER'S LETTER, Mother continued to talk about John coming home. She had the notion that because no personal effects had been returned to her he must be wandering around somewhere with loss of memory. Eventually I came to the conclusion that the only way I could convince her of the inevitable was for me to prove that John was dead. Before leaving India I had written to Major Foster and I asked him if he could tell me the location of the place where John had been killed. This was not perhaps, on reflection, a fair question to ask of him. With the constant movement in wartime he replied to the effect that he was unable to furnish me with precise details. In battle men are usually buried near where they fall, when there is a body to inter, and exact locations for record purposes can be somewhat haphazard depending on the fluidity of a particular action. It is generally left to the War Graves Commission people to trace and exhume the bodies and to locate them in permanent cemeteries. One could well understand, therefore, the War Office's initial reluctance to tell me anything in response to my my enquiry.

However, I persisted and eventually got from them a map reference of the village of St Oedenrode, in Noord Brabant, the Netherlands. With that information available I resolved at the first opportunity to go that place to find his grave.

This occurred in 1945 by which time I had been posted to Germany, to the town of Peine, which lay between the town of Hanover and the British/Russian border crossing point at Helmstedt. I was with a branch of the 70th British Intelligence Division. At that time it was not easy to travel anywhere in Europe, especially in the recently conquered Germany – that country was in almost total ruin and poverty and devastation was to be seen everywhere. There was also a danger in travelling alone from people desperate for food, including many freed slave workers who were in desperate straits and thought nothing of pillaging the countryside of their former oppressors. Nevertheless, I felt I had to make the effort to get to St Oedenrode. While I was considering how best to do this I got talking with a Dutch Sergeant member of our Mess, called Cor Kleintjens. His suggestion immediately solved half my problem. "Oh", he said, "you can go and stay with my wife Anna in Tilburg, it's not far from St Oedenrode". Well, that was a great help because overnight accommodation in a foreign land was an important ingredient to my proposed mission. Colonel Thompson, my Commanding Officer, was only able to grant me three days but wished me luck with my quest.

So with the assurance of accommodation with Anna in Richard Wagner Straat in Tilburg, I planned my trip. Trains were infrequent and unreliable, and with only three days available I felt the best course was to hitch my way there, using one day for the outward journey, one day for the search in St Oedenrode and the final day to return to Germany. It was a very tight schedule and when I come to think of it now I find it difficult to believe I achieved as much as I did in so short a period, especially as a distance of some 280 miles each way was involved.

Peine is adjacent to the autobahn which goes from east to west across Germany. It was built by Hitler in the 1930's not only to provide work for the unemployed but also to facilitate the movement of troops rapidly from east to west. No doubt he was then already thinking of the expansion of Germany and the occupation of neighbouring countries. The autobahn passed Peine, Hanover and continued down into the Ruhr and close to the border of the Netherlands. There was much traffic on the road, mainly allied military vehicles travelling backwards and forwards in the direction of the Netherlands and Belgium. The latter country was then still a convenient place where British messes in Germany could obtain an abundant and varied supply of spirits and champagne to top up the ration.

I realised that my chances of making the journey in one day were quite reasonable. So on a damp, cold November day, the 23rd to be precise, I set out very early. I travelled light with just a haversack containing some coffee which I knew would be very acceptable in the Netherlands, a good supply of cigarettes, which were currency in those days as local money was more or less useless, some sandwiches and a full flask of whisky. It is so long ago now to recall the many vehicles I hitched that day; only one comes to mind. I was getting near to the end of my journey and, having crossed the border into the Netherlands I found myself, in the dark, in the town of Nijmegen. I was lost. In which direction lay Tilburg? In response to my thumb a delivery van stopped and the driver asked if he could help. I managed to make him understand I wished to get on the road to Tilburg. "OK", he replied, and going to the rear of the vehicles opened the small back door and gestured me to get in. There was, I remember, another person inside – a Dutchman I assumed – who greeted me with words I did not understand. Unable to communicate, we sat there in silence. The compartment was small and without ventilation – I was soon aware that it was a cheese van of sorts. The smell of cheese was overpowering, though I don't think my companion was concerned about it for he continued to puff away at his cigar, the smoke from which made the atmosphere stifling. After about fifteen minutes, by which time I was almost breathless, the van came to a halt. The door was opened by the driver who pointed along the road and said "Tilburg" and, gesticulating with his hands, indicated the number of kilometres I had yet to travel. It was clear he could take me no further but I was grateful indeed to be back on the right path. I thanked him and gave him some cigarettes, which pleased him very much for English cigarettes were very popular. In the Netherlands I found the people most helpful; the euphoria of liberation was still with them and it is still remembered even today, fifty years on.

Passing through St Hertogenbosch I eventually reached Tilburg and after several enquiries found Richard Wagner Straat, my refuge for the night. I had been on my journey for about sixteen hours or more and, aching for rest and refreshment, was almost ready to drop. With some trepidation I knocked on the door of Anna's house which was opened by a very attractive, smiling Dutch lady who in her own language invited me to enter. She was aware that I was to visit so was not surprised by my late arrival. She was the mistress of a neat, nicely furnished and sprucely clean home in the fashion of most Dutch houses. She had prepared a meal for me and while I ate she asked after her husband Cor, much of this in sign language. Smiles and gestures answered many questions and we got on famously. At the appropriate hour, not too soon for me, she directed me to a neat and simply furnished bedroom. The comfortable bed was indeed a welcome sight and within minutes of bidding each other goodnight in our own languages I was in a deep and exhausted sleep.

Early next morning Anna tapped on my door and invited me to come and eat breakfast. Imagine my surprise when I reached the table to see a boiled egg at the place where I was to sit. Food was still scarce in the Netherlands following the disastrous damage caused to its agricultural systems during the German occupation – so much of their productive polder land below sea level had been deliberately flooded by the Germans in an attempt to impede the Allied advance. Further, during their retreat from Dutch territory, the German armies ravaged the countryside of its livestock, taking with them on their way to Germany a great number of horses and cattle. The Dutch were left in a parlous state, particularly in the north where the Germans remained in occupation right up to the end of the war in May 1945. Many Dutch people were on the point of starvation, despite the delivery by allied planes of cargoes of food from time to time and many were forced to eat tulip and daffodil bulbs to satisfy their hunger. The situation in those areas liberated in September 1944 was slowly improving but goods were still in very short supply, coffee and tea being two examples. Therefore, to see an egg placed before me was most embarrassing for I was unable adequately to express my appreciation for such a sacrifice. But Anna smiled at my signal efforts of thanks and indicated by sign language that I should eat it before it got cold. She had thoughtfully packed me some sandwiches to sustain me throughout the day because neither of us knew what I would encounter and I needed something to keep me going in that cold November weather.

I made my way early to St Oedenrode – about twenty five kilometres distance – for I was anxious to begin my search, having no idea what I would find when I arrived there.

It was a very cold, damp and misty day, with frequent showers. I eventually reached the town of St Oedenrode and alighted in the marketplace near to the bandstand. The square was deserted which was not surprising, considering the weather. I stood for a few moments feeling something of a fool and wondering "Where do we go from here?"

As I entered the town I had noticed many graves along the roadside. Some were single graves with a rude cross, often topped with a German or British steel helmet, depending on the nationality of the deceased soldier. There were others of two or more together. So I decided to retrace my steps to the outskirts of the town and to work my way back, moving along 'The Corridor' route in the direction of Veghel, and to examine every grave I could find along that road. Most of the dead had been buried presumably near to where they had been killed, as is the usual practice on the battlefield. In one or two instances British soldiers had been buried in the gardens of Dutch houses. One particular grave, a Corporal of the RASC, if I remember correctly, was located in a front garden complete with a kerb surround. It was bedecked with flowers, despite it being winter, and cared for as though it was a family plot. But not so with the German graves, they showed no sign of attention from the local inhabitants. Perhaps this was understandable considering the suffering the Germans had inflicted on the people of many countries in Europe, but they were someone's sons and no doubt many of them had been caught up unwillingly into Hitler's war machine.

Slowly I made my way through the town heading along the main 'Corridor' route since I thought – quite wrongly as it turned out – that John's grave would be somewhere along that highway. It was well past midday, by which time it was raining heavily and I was getting very wet. As I approached the outskirts of the town along Eerschot I saw a Dutchman coming towards me, walking with head bowed against the driving rain. He was dressed in blue working overalls and was wearing clogs, which were all the fashion in those days and which I though quite strange. As he came up to me, recognising my British uniform, he nodded, half smiled and muttered a greeting I did not comprehend. "Ah," I thought, "a friendly native – I'll ask him". So stopping him in his tracks and using a mixture of English and German, and the word panzer to signify I was looking for tanks, I enquired if he knew the location of any tanks of the 44th RTR, and the graves of any of their crews. To his great credit, not mine, he eventually grasped what I was getting at and the reason for my mission to St Oedenrode. This man's name was Ben van Uden and he became a lifelong friend until his death a few years ago.

By this time we were both getting drenched from standing talking in the rain. He beckoned me to accompany him to his nearby home in Eerschot. Perhaps he thought I needed to dry out a little before we began searching for knocked out tanks, for as soon as we entered the house I discovered he wished to offer me food, refreshment and the hospitality of his home.

I was introduced to Oma and Opa, the grandparents, and his dear sister Anna who seemed to run the household – with great efficiency, as I later discovered. She was an excellent cook, too, and showed all my family great kindness when we visited that home on several occasions in 1946, 1947, 1948 and 1950, by which time I had almost become a member of the family.

No sooner had I removed my wet overcoat, which was put before the stove to dry out a little, when Anna asked me if I would like some pap, which to my ear sounded like 'pop'. All of this was in sign language though Anna did have a few words of English. For an Englishman pop meant lemonade and I certainly did not fancy that on a cold winter day – I would much have preferred a hot drink – but not wishing to give offence I nodded assent. To my surprise, after a few minutes in came Anna from the kitchen with a steaming plate of what looked distinctly like porridge and which I found tasty and warming. That, together with Anna Kleintjens' sandwiches, provided me with a nourishing lunch, after which I felt quite fortified against the bleak weather outside.

While I was busily spooning the pap into my mouth both Ben and Anna were trying to relate the excitement they had experienced when the allies had liberated St Oedenrode and especially when some US paratroopers, the first of the allied forces to arrive, had landed near their house. The more they spoke of it the more excited they became; they talked with scorn about the 'Moffa', their derisory term for the Germans. Much of what they said was beyond my comprehension, but the expressions on their faces said it all.

On conclusion of this diversion Ben made me understand that he thought some tanks had been destroyed on the main road out of town in the direction of Veghel. Of course I had no idea where to look and from the many graves of British servicemen I had already seen in that vicinity I was beginning to realise my task was not going to be easy. I later realised that Ben had taken unauthorised time off work at the ODA factory, to which he had been returning when I met him in the street. We set out, tramping in the direction of Veghel and crossing fields whenever we spotted what looked like the graves of allied soldiers. We found many of infantrymen from British regiments, a group of whom, according to the farmer in whose field they were buried, had been burned to death by German flamethrowers. Post war records in St Oedenrode, as prepared by the Red Cross, show that about 150 British servicemen were killed in the area, along with 125 US Paratroopers, eleven of whose names are now recorded for posterity on a plaque in the Market Square of the town. This was erected by the old comrades of 'B' Company of 502 Battalion of the Parachute Infantry Regiment, 101st US Airborne Division.

After about two hours of searching we spotted a tank some hundred yards on the right of the roadside. This was on the land of one Wilhelm van Tanden, at Kempkes, about three or four kilometres from St Oedenrode. Sure enough, it proved to be a tank of the 44th RTR and the farmer pointed out another tank of the same regiment some four hundred yards away near the edge of a wood. This also belonged to the 44th. There was a group of three graves beside each tank, and I recorded the names of the men concerned:

Located 10 yards from farm:
  Lance/Sergeant W W Worley
  Trooper F A Harmans
  Trooper W Robinson

Located 400 yards from farm, near woods:
  Lance/Sergeant T Newman
  Trooper P Hollis
  Trooper F H Huggins

I felt very sad to see those graves, as I imagined that John was in a similar situation and from the condition of the tanks those lads must have met a terrible death. All six men now lie in Uden Cemetery.

By this time it was getting dark and it was obvious we could not continue to search any longer. I felt that I had failed in my mission and my disappointment must have been obvious to Ben as we walked silently back to St Oedenrode. I had to return to Germany the following day for there was no question of overstaying my leave. In hindsight I am sure my Colonel would not have made a fuss, but since one did not as a matter of course overstay one's leave I had not given the possibility a thought. In any case, my visit had made me realise that it might take many days to find a particular grave, for it could be anywhere within the bounds of the town. Those graves we had seen, and there were many, covered a wide area. As it later proved, it took Ben, with local men to assist him, some months before he found the location of John's grave.

We returned to Eerschot to find the family anxiously awaiting the result of our search. Faces were downcast at the news of our failure, but promises were made that they would keep on looking and Ben also promised to make enquiries at the Town Hall. I gave them both my German and home addresses so they could write to me should anything be discovered. I then took my departure from these kind people, doing my best with sign language to express my appreciation for their generous help and hospitality. I departed sadly from St Oedenrode wondering whether the information given by the War Office was correct.

On reaching Tilburg by late evening my disappointment was somewhat dispelled by Anna's kindness and her expression of sorrow at the failure of my mission. She welcomed me back most warmly. In spite of the food shortage she had conjured up an excellent meal which we shared together, for she had awaited my return before eating. After dinner she said we were to go to the house next door, the home of a Mr Witjes and his wife. Anna made me understand that Mr Witjes spoke very good English and would therefore be able to translate our conversation; I think she also wanted a full account of my day in St Oedenrode.

Refreshed and replete after an excellent meal, we headed for next door. There they raised my spirits by plying me with generous measures of Dutch gin and cigars, which were then a very popular smoke in the Netherlands. It seemed all the men puffed away at those enormously fat cigars, and the aroma from them pervaded almost every household. This broke the ice and after I had given them a full account of my trip to St Oedenrode a very pleasant and convivial evening was spent, with Mr Witjes having a busy time acting as interpreter. At one point I detected there was something which was amusing them and I gained the impression it concerned me. They were chuckling away between themselves so I asked Mr Witjes the reason for their amusement. Looking at the two ladies, then back at me, he asked if I thought I had stayed overnight the previous evening alone with Anna. "Why not?" I replied, somewhat puzzled at the question and his translation evoked even more peals of laughter. After this he remarked "And you a British soldier, ha ha. If you had gone into Anna's room during the night you would have had a great shock because I was sleeping in her bed – Anna stayed here with my wife!". I was dumb struck and certainly a little put out, but they were highly amused. I think the real reason for their action – apart from there being a grain of truth as to the activities of (I hope) a minority of their British liberators – was that to the surrounding populace it would certainly have appeared unseemly for a good Dutch lady to accommodate a soldier, or any man for that matter, in her home during the absence of her husband. In my innocence I had not given it a thought. However, I have often smiled to myself about the incident since and wonder whether they too remember my embarrassment.

Anna had a very young daughter at the time. I forget her name but I have a photograph of her taken with me the following morning when we went for a brief walk in the neighbourhood. She was about two or three years old so could now be a mature lady of fifty plus. I do not suppose she recalls our little stroll along the streets of Tilburg.

As I recall, I was able to get a train going some way back into Germany. I took my departure from Anna and her friends, all of whom came to the station to see me off. I had known these people for only a few hours yet here they were treating me like an old friend and Mr Witjes promised to get in touch with Ben van Uden to assist, if required, with the continued search.

As the train meandered slowly through the Netherlands the debris of war was still evident everywhere and tanks and guns, smashed in battle, littered the countryside. But all that faded into insignificance when the train passed through the Arnhem area, which was still exhibiting the mass of crashed gliders in the places where they came to land on that fateful day in September 1944; the clear up had not yet begun. If the Netherlands was bad, Germany was a disaster area, and every railway station and surrounding town was a complete and utter ruin. What a price the German people had paid for the insane ideals of a madman.

I left the train at one of the Ruhr towns, possibly Kleve or Hamm, where that great railway junction was a shambles with only one through line operating. Also the name Recklinghausen comes to mind. Whichever station it was I alighted from I had to make my way to the autobahn, for once on that it was a straight journey back to Peine. Again, I had many lifts. My stock of cigarettes was getting low and I could not afford to tip as generously as I had done on the outward journey, having dispensed with quite a few packets to my new found friends in the Netherlands. For a single English cigarette in those days a German would do almost anything; it was not uncommon for a German to follow you if you were smoking, waiting until you threw your nub end to the floor, then pouncing on it as though it were a gold piece. Very degrading, but strange as it may seem today, tobacco then had a price beyond any other commodity in post war Germany where many a German woman would offer her body for a few cigarettes. Thousands of them had no knowledge of the whereabouts of their menfolk, who had 'disappeared' in their thousands in the Russian campaign. In that country German prisoners of war were not returned home, but often sent to labour camps where they received harsh treatment. However, this was no worse than that meted out to the millions of Russian POWs in German hands, the majority of whom were starved to death, being treated as 'untermenchen' – or sub humans – by their German captors. So many German women, possibly through hunger and the need to feed their 'fatherless' children, made themselves available to their conquerors in the allied zones of occupation. Payment by way of a bar of soap, chocolate or a few cigarettes allowed them to make purchases of black market food. There were, of course, genuine love matches between German girls and allied soldiers who were invariably and sometimes unfairly referred to as 'soap brides'. A marriage to an allied soldier was one way of escaping from the hunger and devastation of their homeland. The German women paid a high price for the sins of their political fathers. Despite the anti-German feeling at the time, following the revelations of the horrors of the concentration camps, one could not but feel sympathy for some individuals, especially those with two or three children whose pinched and pale faces reflected their hunger. They were not the real enemy; they had after all, willingly or otherwise, been duped and brainwashed by an evil political system.

In the Russian zone, however, few women from the very young to the very old were safe from the rampaging of the Soviet soldiery. After the suffering the Germans had so savagely inflicted upon their motherland, they had no conscience as to how they mistreated German women. Rape was rife, especially during and after the closing stages of the war and little concern was shown for other members of the family, husband and children often being present when such barbaric behaviour took place.

My first lift on reaching the autobahn was a vehicle – I believe a British 15 cwt truck – with a German driver. We nearly came to grief for I had not long been aboard, parked on the engine cowling with my back to the windscreen, when the driver, who must have been tired, dozed off. The next thing I knew the truck slewed off the highway and careered along the central reservation knocking down several saplings which had been planted. They were not large or the windscreen would have been smashed and the vehicle seriously damaged, apart from what might have happened to the occupants. It was enough to shake the driver out of his oblivion and to make him take a grip on the wheel and bring the truck back onto the road, which he did with commendable expertise. He did not seem at all perturbed; he was obviously ex-Wermacht and not easily scared. No doubt he had had closer scrapes in his time for he laughed and passed it off as a joke, but I was sufficiently relieved to pass the cigarettes round again. After one or two more short lifts in different vehicles the last one on my journey proved to be the most uncomfortable. This was a German lorry and the cab being full the driver directed me to jump on the back. It was an open truck with a cargo of rough hewn timber which was stacked to the height of the tailboard. So I had to perch myself on the top with my back to the cab as protection against the chill wind which was blowing on that November day. No sooner had we started off than the first few flakes of snow began to fall and in no time at all this developed into a real blizzard. The freezing conditions aboard this open truck, chugging along at forty miles per hour, added to my exhaustion. It took something like two hours to reach the Peine turn off and by this time I was frozen to the marrow and covered in snow. But I was grateful for having been given a lift so gave the driver the remainder of my cigarettes; for heaven knows how I would have fared on that dark autobahn, late at night in midwinter, if he had not stopped. He was profuse in his thanks because the packet of twenty was almost full and to a German that was worth quite a lot.

I made my way down the road by foot, a mile or so, until I

reached the Mess. There I immediately partook of a hot grog to thaw out. Cor Kleintjens was in the Mess and he expressed his regrets at the failure of my mission, but I assured him it had been well worthwhile for at least I had made contact with people who would now do their best to locate John's grave. He was pleased to have news of Anna and his little girl, but I did not mention that part of my visit which had caused my hosts so much amusement.

What I did not realise at the time was that the news of my failure rekindled mother's hopes that John was still alive. This belief was reinforced by a letter from Ben dated December 2nd 1945 written a week after my visit. In it he said that he and thirty local men had searched for the grave without success and that he had also made enquiries to the Red Cross in St Oedenrode who were responsible for registering all fatal battle casualties in the area. They had informed him that they had a record of the names of all allied soldiers buried in St Oedenrode but that John's name was not among them. Ben concluded: 'It is a pity I must tell you that your brother is not killed in St Oedenrode'. I did not hear from Ben again until after I had returned to England to be demobilised from the Army in February 1946. Meanwhile, I had again written to the War Office asking for clarification of the original information given to me which was contrary to that coming from St Oedenrode. The War Office replied to the effect that John's temporary grave in St Oedenrode had been visited by members of the War Graves Commission. At about the same time, it would have been the spring of 1946, I received a further letter from Ben written in Dutch. Not being able to make full sense of it, though I could get the general trend, I realised it was important news as John's name and army number with that of his comrade, Stanley Matthews, was at the end of the letter. Knowing there was in Birmingham a canteen used by members of the Royal Netherlands Army (Marks and Spencer in the High

Street now occupies the site) I went into the City in search of a translator. Within a few minutes I found the help I needed from a Dutch Military policeman, No 300835 K P Plaatsman of the CMP Depot in Birmingham, who with his excellent knowledge of English quickly translated Ben's letter as follows:

Dear George,

Because you have not heard from me for a long time maybe you think I have forgotten you, but that is wrong. Always I have tried to find the grave of your brother and I have had success.

Now I come with a letter to make an end to your anxiety. I feel very sorry for you and your mother but your brother is dead. I have found his grave. I made enquiries in the area where he is buried so that I know exactly how it happened. Now I will let you know it. The tank in which he was in was the first tank on that road and the area was full of Germans. The tank got a direct hit and the driver, his name was Matthews, was killed at once; your brother jumped out of the tank and was directly shot by the Germans, he got a bullet in his head and died instantly. It happened on September 21st 1944 on Thursday afternoon between four and five o'clock. The Germans buried him there at the place itself. I know that because one of the local boys over there helped the Germans to bury him. I have visited his grave yesterday and it was very nicely kept. It was beautiful with flowers – they lay together, Matthews and your brother, but separate.

I hope I have satisfied you so far and I will see to it that your brother's grave is looked after. The place is St Oedenrode, I think you still know it, between the two big towns Eindhoven and St Hertogenbosch, and it is very easily reached. Here follows the inscription on the crosses of your brother and his comrade Matthews:

No. 7946671 Tpr Thorogood J F
44 RTR 21.9.1944

To Lay the Ghost

No. 7946103 Tpr S Matthews
44 RTR 21.9.1944

Ben

Plaatsman expressed his condolences and I thanked him for his helpful assistance.

Mother was immediately acquainted with this news, which she accepted with resignation. I believe she would rather have clung to her earlier belief for the arrival of Ben's letter meant there was no longer, even for her, any hope of John's return.

At this time I was about to rejoin my former unit in Germany which was becoming civilianised under the Foreign Office (German Section) and was to employ many multi-lingual civilian officers, many of whom had worked at Bletchley during the war, where the German Enigma Code had been broken. Knowledge of the Code gave Britain an insight into all German signal traffic. In passing on information gleaned from the knowledge that Britain exclusively had access to, she had to be careful not to alert the Germans to the fact that their vital code was known to the enemy. This gave Britain and her allies a distinct advantage over an unsuspecting enemy in the conduct and outcome of the war. Additionally, many bilingual Dutch people were engaged for the specialised work of our Branch. I had been recruited as a Control Commission Officer responsible for all aspects of administration concerning the British element of which there were some four hundred or more on strength.

Following its defeat, Germany was divided into four zones of occupation; the largest, in the east, was occupied by the Russians, while some western and southern areas were divided between the French and the United States. Great Britain, whose region included the most devastated areas of Germany, was responsible for the Ruhr, North Rhine Westphalia and Schleswig Holstein, with the US having the Bremen Enclave to provide them with port facilities. It was at that time predicted by the powers that be, and generally understood by all those serving there, that Germany would be occupied by the allies for many years to come. So my return to Germany would give me the opportunity to revisit St Oedenrode. Shortly before leaving for Germany I received a second important letter from Ben, dated June 14th 1946:

My Dear Friend George,

Because I have some important news for you I want to write you a letter. First, George, many heartiest thanks for the second parcel which you have sent. I become it on 11th June, 1946. As soon as time is better I hope to send you some things back, but now it is impossible for me.

And now the news. The 12th June forenoon about 10 o'clock your brother was exhumed and brought to an English cemetery – to a small village named Uden, about 15km (10 miles) north east from St Oedenrode. I already knew that the English soldiers were exhuming in our village, so I told to the people near the grave to warn me as soon as they came. S Matthews, at the time burned to death, as I've written you, he was nearly perished but your brother was about the same as the first day he died, clothes and shoes all in good order – and round his neck he beared a medal with his name on it I think. The soldiers took this with them.

Though your brother is away here, we are still waiting for you. Perhaps we have thought you will come now Whitsuntide. George you come to St Oedenrode, we go together to Uden where your brother is now. And we sure go to the place where he was killed, I know that correctly. The tank is still there. About ten times I have been to the photographer but not at any time he had films, otherwise we had taken photographs of the graves. If possible George please to write when you will come to see us. You will be our guest. You can eat and sleep here. With your English letters I go to the Head of the (Grammar) elementary school here. He finds out and explains it to me. Everything is very easy if you know the way I see. Many greetings and kind regards to your mother and wife and yourself. From your very sincere friend –

Ben

At the first opportunity after returning to Peine I planned to go to St Oedenrode and it must have been late summer when I made my way there. My journey on that occasion was in comfort; direct by train via Utrecht to St Hertogenbosch and then by regular bus to St Oedenrode, where I was accommodated at the hospitable home of the van Uden family. Knowing of the acute shortage of foodstuffs in the Netherlands I took with me a suitcase full of rare commodities such as tea, coffee, some tinned goods like ham and bully beef and a good supply of cigarettes. To obtain all these things I scrounged from friends and was also helped by our friendly Captain Quartermaster who contributed a few items from his 'surplus' stock, which quartermasters always seem to have available.

It was late afternoon when I reached Eerschot, where I was warmly received. Much had happened during the preceding ten months or so. Conditions in the Netherlands were slowly improving but food and beverages were still in short supply so the gasps of pleasure when the suitcase of goodies was opened gave me much satisfaction and I felt the inconvenience of carrying all that weight had been worthwhile. The coffee and tea were particularly welcome even though the coffee was not of the ground variety to which the Dutch are particularly partial. After some light refreshment Ben suggested we should go to what I now know to be de Ollandseweg where the action took place which resulted in the deaths of many soldiers from both sides, although the majority were enemy dead. On the way we passed three graves of US paratroopers who were buried in a lane at the rear of a row of cottages. I thought it somewhat incongruous to see a full set of false teeth lying on top of one of the graves.

About a mile along de Ollandseweg we saw the wrecked tank lying at an angle, its left track in the ditch, on the left hand side of the road. It had come to a halt right up against a large oak tree which had stopped its uncontrolled progress after being hit by anti-tank fire. The tree was badly burned when the tank went up in flames, and later on it was removed and a new sapling planted. Oddly, the replacement tree over many years has failed to grow at the same rate as other new trees planted in the area.

The tank hatches were open. I entered the wrecked vehicle from the gunners hatch, trying whilst doing so to imagine how anyone could extricate themselves from such a small aperture – especially in a battle situation with bullets flying around. I found the interior claustrophobic in the extreme and, as can be imagined, it was a shambles. In the fire all the ammunition had exploded causing great havoc and burning everything ignitable to cinder – what a Dantes' inferno it must have been. The floor of the tank was strewn with all the metallic debris of ammunition cases and projectiles, and heaven only knows what remnants of equipment which would only be recognizable to a Trooper. How anyone could live and fight in such a confined space was beyond me, for there was so little room for manoeuvre. Surprisingly, tank men preferred their environment to that of the infantrymen who, in their view, were more vulnerable outside the comparative safety of their armoured monsters. There was some truth in that belief for the casualty rate in front line infantry regiments was far higher than that in armoured formations. For example, the 4th Dorsets, after sustaining heavy casualties in their first engagement with the enemy in Normandy, went into the attack on the village of Maltot, south of Caen, against determined opposition from a

Panzer division. In that battle the whole of their 'A' company was lost; not a man returned. Also, two thirds of their remaining three companies were casualties and three company commanders were all missing.

Inside the tank the body of poor Stanley Matthews, the driver, had remained for some weeks – from the position of the German shells he must have been killed instantly. One of the shots had pierced the mantel directly in front of the driver's seat while the second shot was a little way to the left, but both were accurate and either would have proved fatal to the driver. Our activity around the tank encouraged several local men to join us and a conversation developed between Ben, Anna and these men, who obviously knew something about what had happened two years previously. I now know them to be members of the van Weert family, opposite whose home the tank had come to rest. Unfortunately, there was no interpreter among us so most of the discussion was in sign language, but I managed to understand something of what had occurred. They obviously did not want to go into too much detail in an attempt to spare my feelings. One of the men was Dorus van Weert, who had been ordered by the Germans to bury John. This was done in the evening of September 21st at about 8pm, after the fighting had subsided, when his body was placed in a German slit trench. While the men were talking Anna went to a nearby farmhouse and returned with a US-type water bottle which the farmer said he had taken out of the tank and used as a drinking vessel while working on the land. It was dented and blackened in many places showing how it must have been damaged by the exploding ammunition inside the tank. I remonstrated with Anna as I did not wish to deprive the farmer of his container, but she insisted I keep it as a souvenir. I still have it.

Shortly before we left I noticed Anna and Ben in an earnest conversation with the van Weert brothers, of which I could understand nothing as they were speaking rapidly in Dutch. From the expressions on their faces it seemed as though they were talking about something concerning John which it was preferable I did not know, but I felt I had to enquire what it was that concerned them and I asked Anna to explain. Looking somewhat sorrowful Anna, hesitatingly, told me that as he lay on the ground after he had been shot, John had called out 'Mother, Mother'. How long it took for him to die they did not say and I had not the courage to ask. I never revealed this to mother, for it would have haunted her for the rest of her life.

That visit to de Ollandseweg was a very emotional moment for me, particularly when Ben showed me the spot in the nearby field where John and Stan had lain side by side for almost two years. Walking slowly back to the village with Ben and Anna I pondered upon my visit the next day to Uden, when at long last I would be near to John again. How I wish I could have spoken freely to my good companions to thank them adequately for all they had done to assist me in my quest. But I am sure they knew how much I appreciated their kindness and valued the help they had given me since I first entered their home in November 1945.

Next day after breakfast the three of us went by regular bus from St Oedenrode up 'The Corridor' route via Veghel, scene of the heavy fighting in September 1944 when the Germans made several attempts to breach the vital line of communication up which travelled all the supporting units of 30 Corps, until we reached the small town of Uden. The Uden War Cemetery is located about four hundred yards from the centre of the town, on the Nijmegen road at its junction with the road to Zeeland. It was formerly a Roman Catholic cemetery which had fallen into disuse and was acquired in 1943 by the Municipality of Uden for the internment of many British and Commonwealth airmen whose planes over the war years had crashed in that vicinity on their return from bombing raids over Germany. Of the total of

695 allied dead in the cemetery, 255 are of the Royal Air Force, the majority being British (but with eighteen Australians and seven New Zealanders), which gives an indication of the very high casualty rate in Bomber Command. Many of those airmen had been buried, prior to their reinterment in Uden Military Cemetery, in a temporary graveyard in the garden of the local Roman Catholic priest. Those graves during the war years, of which I have since seen many photographs, were beautifully tended and regularly bedecked with flowers. My good friend in Uden, Jan Heesen of St Annastraat, had been responsible throughout the war (when in the employ of the local council) for the collection, registration and burial of those unfortunate flyers with the able assistance of that caring priest. After the war Jan held the post of Secretary of the Nederlands Oorlogsgraven Comite in Uden.

On that day in 1946, my first visit, just plain metal white crosses marked the graves and among the newly turned earth one could see the odd small human bone belonging to the former inhabitants of Uden whose remains had previously occupied that plot. It was a sombre moment as I stood before John's grave. Looking down at that simple cross I noticed an incorrect initial had been painted – an E instead of an F – as if it really mattered. I found it difficult to believe that like so many other brave young men who had suffered the fears and horrors of war, beneath my feet at some unknown depth lay the mutilated body of my dear John. I tried to picture him there, but all I could see was as I last saw him in January 1940, standing on the platform at New Street Station with his arm protectively around mother's shoulder and waving me goodbye with a smile as the train slowly gathered speed to part us forever. As I took my leave of him I promised myself that I would return to this hallowed spot. I felt also that at long last my mission had been fulfilled and I knew that his final resting place was among friendly and caring people. That was a great consolation to both mother and myself.

I remained with my hosts for about a week and we went to Uden several times. On one occasion we were accompanied by Opa, the old grandfather, who kindly put on his best suit. At the end of the week I said my thanks and goodbyes to the van Uden family and in response to their insistence promised I would bring mother in 1947. It was not easy at that time for civilians to travel abroad from the UK for there were not all the facilities for travel which are so readily available today. But I had it in mind that by hook or by crook I would get mother over to the Netherlands as soon as it was feasible.

This did occur in June 1947, when we made the journey together to St Oedenrode. How the family welcomed us, treating mother with great kindness and consideration. She had purchased for Ben a hallmarked silver cigarette case, engraved with his initials as a token of thanks for what he had done, and also brought gifts for the rest of the family.

We made several visits to Uden. They were indeed sad moments for both of us, but for mother especially. As always, she showed great courage and fortitude and bore up very well. On each occasion that we visited the cemetery she sat there for some time for she seemed to want to absorb the memory of that place to take back home with her. By now it was like a beautiful garden with well tended lawns interspersed with shrubs and flowers which bloomed in the beds between the crosses.

I tried to avoid taking her to de Ollandseweg because I thought visiting the cemetery was enough for her to cope with, but she insisted as she wanted to see the place in the field where the boys had been buried. Fortunately, the tank was no longer there, having been broken up for scrap some months earlier. However, we met a young girl called Toni van Hommel (now a mature married lady by the name of van Cuijk) who lived nearby and who, whilst they were there, had regularly placed flowers upon the graves. It gave mother additional comfort to learn of the kindness of such a young girl and this reinforced her belief that John's final resting place was among worthy people.

His last two letters were sent to mother and myself, both dated September 16th 1944 and written, I assume, during the brief respite from battle in the town of St Nicholas in Belgium. He said to mother:

> Yes dear, I am looking after myself so there is no need to worry over me. God has smiled on me so far as George said, and I have my trust in Him, so chin up old girl and keep that smile there, for that is all I shall look for when I am home again.

To me he wrote:

> Well, George, I suppose you have heard on the news what a great welcome we are getting out here now. The people are going mad with joy, and it makes this fighting a bit better when you know the people really want you.

Among John's few possessions was found a card which mother had sent to him which he had carried throughout his service in North Africa, Sicily and Italy. He left it behind in a wallet when he went to France with the invasion forces. It said:

> GOD
> *Bless my dear and all his ways*
> *Oh follow him through dangerous days*
> *And bring him back from anywhere*
> *With your help and loving care*

We stayed in St Oedenrode for about ten days and it was quite an experience for mother, for apart from a visit to Paris in 1926 she had never before been abroad. It was also new to live with such a large family as the van Udens', when so many came to pay their respects to Oma and Opa after church on Sunday. Then the house was packed with chattering children and grandchildren, all dressed in their Sunday best. This was something quite new to us, coming as we did from a small family with no immediate relatives. We also saw the old ladies in their distinctive Brabant costumes with their wide brimmed hats, going to and from church. It was all very engaging. We visited with Anna a local clog factory; I think it was along de Ollandseweg. There we watched a pair of clogs being made by hand from a solid block of wood, which was an intriguing operation, and we were pleased to receive the clogs as a gift. Unfortunately, with the passing of the years, and the use of more modern footwear few such factories now exist.

Another day we took Anna to Amsterdam for a day out, where we dined at one of the best hotels. It was our way of showing a little appreciation to Anna, on whose shoulders rested all the responsibility for the household chores; she was tireless in her efforts to make our stay pleasant and we ate like royalty at Eerschot. How she managed to conjure up such delicious food was beyond us.

We were introduced to spek – raw smoked bacon which was home cured from their own pigs which were raised in a sty in the back garden. They also preserved their own vegetables and fruit, and the cellar beneath the house by this time was packed from floor to ceiling with bottled goods. From the ceiling itself hung joints of spek. When a fresh supply for table was required Anna would cut off a chunk and have the local butcher slice it wafer thin on his bacon machine. Anna also took a supply of sugar, flour and cream to the local bakery and she would return there some hours later to collect a batch of varied and delicious cakes, the like of which we never saw in England. We lived far better than the rations in the UK or Germany would allow, but I suppose it was easier for country people anywhere to fare that much better than those in the larger towns. The van Udens were undoubtedly thrifty people so far as food was concerned and had quickly recovered from the immediate post-war shortage, though we did wonder what sacrifice to their stock of goods they had made in order to cater for us so generously. A monetary contribution was offered, but this was bluntly refused – they seemed genuinely happy to accommodate and feed us and we certainly enjoyed their hospitality and company.

We were surprised at the economy in the use of tableware. After our plate of soup had been consumed the main course was served onto the same dish and a lump of fresh bread was supplied to wipe your plate ready to receive the pudding. All very practical, we thought, though we never managed to adapt to the habit ourselves; it certainly saved a lot of washing up.

Mother and I revisited St Oedenrode in 1948, again at our own expense; the War Office gave no financial assistance for such pilgrimages unless one could prove 'pecuniary need' and who would wish to ask for charity? On each of mother's visits the Knight Optical Company gave her a generous sum contributed by the staff which she used to purchase flowers for John's grave. A letter from the Manager, Mr S Smith, read:

Dear Mrs Thorogood,

We hear that you are visiting the Netherlands next week for the purpose of visiting your son Jack's grave and we wish you a pleasant journey and that you will enjoy your stay with the friends who are very carefully and loyally tending the sacred spot. It is the wish of the entire staff that you obtain a floral bouquet or wreath on our behalf to the memory of our dear pal Jack who was so well loved and admired by all who came into contact with him. His name will live forever amongst his friends and we trust that you will have some small consolation in having seen and visited his last resting place.

Leaving St Oedenrode, mother accompanied me to Hamburg, where I was then stationed, for an extended holiday. In 1949 I made a similar visit with my wife, Ivy, who had known John very well having worked with him on the ARP post in Grove Lane. On that occasion we were accompanied by our baby daughter, Gillian. What a fuss the van Udens made of her! In case we needed anything they had furnished a special room for her with a cot, bed linen and baby clothes borrowed from among members of the family who had young children – we were most impressed with the trouble they had taken over this. Again, it was a most pleasant occasion despite the reason for our being there and the family went to a great deal of trouble to make our stay as enjoyable as possible. They also hosted a visit from my mother-in-law, who had journeyed to Belgium to meet a notable family who had befriended her twenty two year old son Douglas when he passed through Turnhout at the time the 4th Dorsets were advancing into that country. She also had known John well and wished to visit his grave.

My visit in 1950 was to be my last for many years for in February 1951 I returned with my family to England, the role of the Control Commission having come to an unexpected end. This resulted from the USSR granting self government to East Germany, albeit as a communist regime answerable to the Soviet Union. The action of the USSR precipitated the Western Powers, the United States, Great Britain and France into following suit. So with Western Germany regaining its autonomy the run down of the Control Commission began in earnest and thus ended what had been thought to be a long engagement. With the need to resettle in England after an absence of twelve years and to provide for a growing family my finances, unfortunately, did not stretch to visits abroad.

More Dutch Hospitality

IMAGINE MOTHER'S SURPRISE WHEN EARLY IN 1961 SHE RECEIVED A LETTER from the Netherlands War Graves Committee inviting her to the Netherlands as a guest of the Committee. This was heartwarming indeed, for no such help had ever been offered by an official body in Britain. By 1961 mother had reached the age of seventy nine and although still very active and working happily at the Knight Optical Company she was too frail to undertake such a journey alone. So I wrote to the Committee asking if I could accompany her, explaining the reason for this and also offering to pay my own expenses. Almost by return of post came a reply to the effect that I would be equally welcome as their guest and that no monetary contribution would be required from me. Our hearts warmed yet again to the Dutch people. We left Birmingham on May 25th 1961 and stayed overnight at the Station Hotel in Liverpool Street – I think it cost something in the region of four pounds each with breakfast extra, which is quite a difference to today's prices. The next day we travelled to Harwich to catch the ferry for the sea journey to the Hook-of-Holland. The day crossing proved to be very rough, sufficiently so to get a mention in the newspaper which reported our arrival in the Netherlands. We reached our destination, the town of Nijmegen – scene of great activity during 'Market Garden' – in the afternoon and were met at the station by representatives of the Committee. From the station we were conveyed by coach to an hotel where we had light refreshments. This was followed by introductions to our host families with whom we were to be accommodated during the long weekend of our stay. Mother was paired with Fred and Riki Rohn and I with Toin and Mimi van Ooyen – both of these families lived in Ballotstraat so we were conveniently near each other.

Fred Rohn was a very active member of the Committee, who were responsible for the arrangements for the visiting British 'pilgrims' (as we were known) to stay with local people who provided free accommodation. Despite this, there were still meals at the hotel to be paid for in addition to the cost of trips and entertainment. Most of the money for the fund was raised by collections in the Nijmegen area. Fred, for example, collected money each week from his workmates when they received their pay packets. This enabled the Committee to offer visits to relatives who came from all corners of the Commonwealth. To us Brits, who in the main received nothing from our own Government, this was quite a remarkable effort on the part of those generous Dutch people, so it was to Fred that I put the question: 'Why do you do it?' This stopped him in his tracks. He turned to me and said: 'We in the Netherlands will never forget our liberation and the debt we owe to those who gave their lives for our freedom. Only those who have been occupied by the Germans can understand what freedom means to us'. As an afterthought he commented, 'Remember; you in England never experienced the loss of freedom'. Thirty two years later I became aware through my visit to the Kienehoefschool in St

Oedenrode that such sentiments still exist despite the passing of the years.

We were told an amusing story by Mimi van Ooyen concerning British troops who were billeted in their home for some days during the fighting in the Nijmegen area in the Autumn of 1944. She said they got on famously and the soldiers shared their food with them. When they learned she had no winter coat one of the soldiers gave her a blanket. At the first opportunity she cut it out to a pattern, put her sewing machine on the table and began stitching the various pieces together.

Whilst busily and happily engaged in this pursuit her concentration was interrupted by the arrival of an officer who walked into the room, ostensibly to speak to his men. His presence terrified Mimi because she did not know what his reaction would be to seeing a British Army blanket being so misused. He didn't miss it – in fact it was apparent that he had immediately spotted what was going on. For a moment or two he looked first at the blanket and then at Mimi, the severity reflected in his face adding to her fears. Slowly he walked across the room to the table where she was working, took a piece of the cloth between thumb and forefinger and, with a smile creasing his countenance, said 'Nice bit of stuff', or words to that effect. The relief Mimi felt was unbounded, for she had fully expected to be arrested or punished for the crime of misusing British equipment. The officer turned from her, still smiling, to give orders to his men, who were also amused at her embarrassment. Nothing more was said and no reprimand was given, as far as she knew, to the soldier who had donated the blanket to a young and needy Dutch girl.

Whilst we breakfasted with our host family, all other meals (which were excellent) were provided at the Hotel Erica. Visits were arranged by coach to Arnhem, crossing the now famous John Frost Bridge, named after the Commanding Officer of the

2nd Parachute Battalion who so gallantly attempted to hold the bridge against overwhelming odds until relief came. As history records, it did not come, but the stand of the 2nd Parachute Battalion is now part of the history of Arnhem, along with the bravery of the British, allied forces and local Dutch people who took part in that débâcle. Then we moved on to the dropping zones where the 1st British Airborne Division had landed on September 17th, followed by a boat trip on the Neder Rijn and a chair-lift ride which overlooked much of the battle area. On Sunday morning there was held a most moving memorial service in the local Jonkerboss Military Cemetery. There an eighty three year old man, Mr Hunter (who had lost five of his seven sons in two world wars), laid a wreath of poppies on the grave of one of his boys. A very proud man, he stood up to the ordeal very well and was very popular with everyone.

The service at the Jonkerboss was attended by a Dutch Male Voice Choir and representatives of the Nijmegen branch of the Royal British Legion. It was a very solemn occasion and for many in our party it was the first time of visiting the grave of a loved one so emotions were high. There were few dry eyes when the Dutch Padre spoke movingly about the sacrifices made by the allied servicemen buried in his country. The minute's silence, a time for personal thoughts, was a moment one does not easily forget.

On Monday, Fred Rohn kindly took me and mother by car to Uden – it had been thirteen years since mother was last there. Pleased though she was to have been given the opportunity to be near to her dear John once more, she was saddened by the realisation that this might be for her the last time and it was with some reluctance that she departed from the cemetery. As always, outwardly she gave little sign of her grief; there were never any hysterics – that was not her way. That was not British, she would say.

More Dutch Hospitality

Our visit to Nijmegen was reported in the newspaper TROUW on Monday 29th May 1961, with a photograph of mother in company with Fred and Riki Rohn and an account of the reason for her visit. That evening, which was our last before we were to board the train for the homeward journey, the Dutch entertained us at a most enjoyable gathering at a local hotel. All guests and their hosts were present, there was much fun and laughter and our Dutch friends made every effort to round off our visit with something to remember. Both Mr Hunter and mother were presented with gifts, they being the oldest male and female guests. Mr Hunter was given a table lamp in the form of a Dutch boat and mother received a leather handbag. Both gifts were presented by Den Heer Goetzen, Chairman of the Netherlands War Graves Committee.

One of the highlights of the trip for me had been trying to negotiate my way through the 'Flying Dutchman' housed in a building in the grounds of the Hotel Erica. The interior of this was designed to represent the deck of a ship on a rough sea, with the decks at a forty five degree angle. Trying to walk through it was a new and very difficult experience. It was a very popular attraction and I am surprised that (to my knowledge) nobody has copied it and brought it over to England.

We left Nijmegen on Tuesday evening and were seen off by our new found friends. The platform was crowded and when the time came to bid goodbye to those generous people it was not without some signs of emotion. For mother that visit was a crowning moment in her difficult life. It made a lasting impression on her and she often spoke about it. Sadly she died, after a short illness, in the early spring of 1961, but that trip to the Netherlands brought her much contentment during the closing days of her life. She returned home with the belief that many people in that small country really cared about the young men who had found their final resting place in Dutch soil.

Five years elapsed before I revisited the Netherlands. This was in 1966 when my wife and I with our two sons, John and Neil, motored via France and Belgium, visiting St Nicholas on the way. There we parked our car in the market square and ate a picnic lunch. It was a pleasant day with a cloudless sky. Watching the locals busily engaged making their purchases from the market stalls we wondered if any of them had been present in the square when the 44th liberated the town. Now all was peaceful and what we were seeing was a prosperous community going happily about their daily business. We continued our journey until we reached St Oedenrode. There we pitched our tent among the trees on a wooded campsite nearby de Ollandseweg. Fifteen years had passed since we had been in St Oedenrode and we received a great welcome from the van Uden family. Many of the young children had reached maturity and we found difficulty in recognising them; there were, in any case, so many in that large family that it was impossible to remember them all.

We went to Uden on several occasions and also made various trips to places of interest. We took Ben's two boys, Ad and Benny, to De Efterling, a popular amusement park and also visited the Openlucht Museum in Arnhem. The latter is one of the best of its kind I have ever seen, comprising a wide range of exhibits reflecting the style of life lived by Dutch people over the centuries.

I must recount an amusing incident which took place outside Nijmegen railway station. I had just parked my car, with the intention of going to a local bank to change some travellers cheques, when there was a tap on the window. I looked to see an excited Dutchman, his face wreathed in a wide grin and almost jumping for joy. Somewhat nonplussed I wound down the window to be greeted with the gesticulating Dutchman saying excitedly 'We're beating them, we're beating them!' I thought he was mad and asked him what he was talking about. His face dropped, he looked astounded and then recovering he somewhat shamefacedly said, 'The World Cup; we're beating the Germans, England is winning'. He looked at me with amazement on his face as I replied somewhat lamely 'Oh, are we?' Not being a football fan, even at World Cup level, my indifference must have deflated that poor man as he turned and walked away, shaking his head in disbelief. He had obviously spotted our GB number plate and wished to share in what he believed would be our delight at such a victory. No doubt he was thinking that the English were really as mad as is the popular belief abroad and I have often wondered what he told his family and friends about that encounter with a stupid Englishman on World Cup day 1966.

The matter did not finish there. We had decided to take the opportunity whilst in Nijmegen to visit Fred and Riki Rohn and the van Ooyen family. After changing the cheques we went to Ballotstraat only to find that Fred and Riki were not at home, so we went to the van Ooyen household just five doors away. We knocked on the door at a very inappropriate moment, for the family were all engrossed with watching the last fifteen minutes of the match. They let us in with the briefest of greetings then quickly went back to their chairs to gaze excitedly at the television screen for the closing stages of the match. There we sat, four English people watching with only a semi interested air their national team playing a winner against the Germans. The Dutch, on the other hand, sitting on the edge of their chairs, were screaming their heads off with excitement. When it came to the final winning goal you would have thought it was their own national team which had scored. I think the rest of the afternoon was spent discussing that great match, the Dutch people being the main participants in the conversation.

To our surprise the following day, on returning to our tent

after another day out we found a note left by Fred Rohn who had travelled with Riki from Nijmegen to see us. It was unfortunate that we had been absent, but we did manage to see them before we left for England.

The weather during our two week stay was atrocious for it rained almost every day. The sandy soil added to the discomfort since the wet sand carried into the tent, stuck to our shoes, and made our living quarters somewhat messy. We were invited several times to the van Uden home for a meal and spent many a convivial evening in their company.

Some years later, in 1969, Ben and his wife Nettie, together with Ad and Benny, visited England for a two week stay. I travelled to London and met them from the boat train from Harwich. Before returning to Solihull they were given a tour of London which culminated in a visit to the Tower of London. This impressed them very much, especially the crown jewels.

This visit we saw as an opportunity to repay the hospitality they had shown my family on many occasions and we set to with a will to show them a good time. We made a tour of North Wales, visiting Harlech Castle and many of the beauty spots in that area. Several trips were made to the Cotswolds; Blenheim Palace and Bladen to see Churchill's grave occupied another day; while Warwick and Kenilworth Castles and Stratford-upon-Avon also featured on the agenda.

A great event which happened during their time with us was the sharing of that moment in history when Neil Armstrong first set foot on the moon. The prepared lunch on June 21st 1969 got cold because nobody wanted to miss seeing man take his first step on terra firma in space.

Of all the people we would have liked to entertain Anna, sadly, never came to England. For most of the years her role in life was to care for her ageing parents. Later on she did write to say she could come, accompanied by her nephew Benny, but regrettably her dates clashed with a visit we were making to Canada. When we invited her again she would not undertake the journey alone, for Benny was no longer available to escort her. I think she was a little nervous and could not bring herself to travel so far alone, which was a great pity because she really deserved a holiday and it would have given us great pleasure to play host to her for a change.

Many years passed before those places in the Netherlands were revisited. Then in 1979 my brother-in-law, Douglas, mentioned that he had a wish to go over his old battle ground in Europe. First he wanted to go to Normandy to see the place where he had landed with the 4th Dorsets and to follow their route through France, Belgium, the Netherlands and up into Germany. Having a car and tent trailer – ideal for the purpose since they would give us mobility – I suggested we follow this plan. I too was interested, for the activities of the 44th RTR had been closely involved in several battles in support of Doug's Division, the 43rd Wessex.

We set off on the night of May 27th, our trailer displaying both the Divisional and Regimental signs which Doug had so professionally prepared. When we got abroad the signs attracted many a toot on a car horn, followed by a thumbs up sign – an indication that there were still people about who remembered.

Crossing from Folkstone to Boulogne we travelled along the coast road passing through the Etaples area. Etaples is well known for both the huge First World War Commonwealth Cemetery and also famous – or infamous if you give credence to the story of the Monocled Mutineer – for the large number of camps, including the notorious 'Bull Ring' where reinforcements for 'the Front' were subjected to severe and rigorous training. This was to prepare them to face the frightful conditions of trench warfare. Passing through the sandy scrubland it was difficult to believe it was a place where thousands upon thousands of soldiers were pushed to the limits of their endurance; to be fed into the machine consigning men to their early deaths.

We stayed overnight at the nearby camp site and took the opportunity of visiting the cemetery. For the first time visitor to a military cemetery, Etaples Commonwealth War Cemetery in the Pas de Calais is a most dramatic and thought provoking experience. It is situated on the high ground on the right of the coast road, D940, from Boulogne to Abbeville. The entrance is flanked by two imposing towers overlooking the lower burial ground which stretches seawards like a huge Roman ampitheatre. This gives a dominating panoramic view of all the eleven thousand graves in what is the second largest World War I cemetery in France. The great majority of men buried there died of wounds and disease in the many base hospitals which were situated in that area, which means that most of the dead lie in named graves.

A total of thirty five Commonwealth countries are represented by the dead in Etaples Cemetery, a reflection of the contribution which the old Empire countries made to the conflict in France. There are also a number of German war dead buried there in their separate plots. No doubt they were also casualties who were treated in British hospitals. What we found to be most strange was the relatively large number of coolies of the Chinese Labour Corps buried there and we wondered why these people left their homeland to work for a pitiful wage in such atrocious conditions in Flanders. Perhaps conditions in their own country made the prospects of working in Europe attractive.

On reaching Arromanche, where the 4th Dorsets landed, Doug went down to the beach and walked out seawards. He was attempting to get his bearings on the spot where he had disembarked from his seaborne craft on that eventful day thirty five years earlier. I expect it was a very special moment for him and one in which I could not share. He recalled that of all his Company who landed on that day, only he and two others were still with the Battalion when the war ended in Germany some eleven months later. He himself had been wounded twice during that time and returned to duty after being discharged from hospital in England. He regarded himself as extremely lucky to have survived the war.

The remnants of the Mulberry harbour – those huge concrete casements which had made up the artificial port for the landing of vehicles, supplies and troops – were still to be seen. Like massive decaying molars they jutted up from the sea bed while the water gently lapped against their barnacled and ageing façades. Above it all on the high ground an Organisation Todt-built observation post, once part of Hitler's Atlantic Wall, continues to dominate the scene although it is now used as a tourist attraction and information bureau.

A visit to the site of a German heavy gun battery at Longues, overlooking the Normandy beaches, was another significant reminder for Doug. He explained that the last time he had been in one of those gun positions in June 1944 he had seen hanging from the concrete wall the arm of a German soldier, a blast having blown the rest of the body to kingdom come.

Our route took us to Pegasus Bridge, scene of the gallant operation led by Major John Howard of the Ox and Bucks Light Infantry. The task given to Major Howard in the early hours of June 6th 1944 was to seize the two bridges about five hundred yards apart – the first over the Canal de Caen and the second over the River Orne near the village of Bennouville. With the bridges secured the allied assault forces on the Normandy beach head would be able to link up with the 6th British Airborne Division which had secured the eastern flank. The company, supported by a troop of Royal Engineers making a total of 180 men, were transported in six Horsa gliders, four of which landed alongside the northern edge of the canal bank in what was later described as one of the most skilful navigational and flying achievements of the war. The result was a complete surprise to the Germans, who were soundly defeated after a brisk engagement. The losses sustained by Major Howard's force were two killed and several wounded. These were among the first casualties of the Normandy campaign, Lieutenant H D Brotheridge who led the initial charge cross the canal bridge being the first man to fall from a fatal burst of machine gun fire. He is buried beneath the wall of the Ranville church with many other early airborne casualties.

With both bridges secured by Major Howard's Company, they dug in and held their positions until reinforced by men of the 7th Battalion the 5th Parachute Brigade, who suffered grievous losses defending the bridges. Just after dawn Lord Lovat's 1st Special Services (Commando) Brigade passed through, led by the Lord himself accompanied by his personal piper, Bill Millin, who had some hours earlier piped the commandos ashore to the tune of *Highland Laddie*.

Our route took us through such places as Cheaux, Gavrus, Everecy, and Hills 113 and 112, where the 44th RTR had also seen heavy fighting and had lost many men and tanks. At every British cemetery, starting with Bayeux, Doug quietly walked along the rows looking for the graves of his many comrades who had fallen when serving with the 4th Dorsets. We travelled through France, Belgium and the Netherlands, visiting all those places he remembered as being particularly sticky.

On we journeyed up to the northern part of the Netherlands to a place called Borne, near to the German border where he said he might try to find a Dutch lass who had befriended him when his regiment had taken the town after very severe fighting. However, I thought that was being a little too hopeful and eventually convinced him not to pursue his ghost of the past.

Doug said that immediately following the liberation the Town Council had renamed the marketplace 'Dorsetplein' in honour of their victory. We looked for it but could not find it. We approached a Dutchman who was standing on the doorstep of a nearby house, and who seemed to be interested in our activities, and asked him if he could point out 'Dorsetplein'. He replied in good English; 'You have your car parked on it and have been standing on it for the past half hour!' Well, that did surprise us, especially when we found that it had long since been renamed after a member of the Dutch Royal Household. Ah well, you can't win them all.

Another memorable moment was when we crossed over the border into Germany and made a special visit to a place where the Battalion had been engaged heavily and had lost many men. This was what was known as the Sittard Triangle, formed by the towns of Nierdebusch, Geilenkirken and Neinsburg. The particular action has been named in *History of the 4th Dorsets* as 'Dorset Wood' which was opposite the village of Tripsrath.

The wood, when we reached it, was surrounded by a high wire fence with 'Keep Out' notices in German prominently displayed at intervals advising that it was dangerous to enter. Doug, not to be put off, decided that he would risk all that in an attempt to try to find his old slit trench. In this, apparently, he had quite a terrifying experience. He was alone in the trench in a forward observation position in front of his platoon, a solitary sentry with orders to keep his eyes and ears open for any signs of the enemy. The silence of the night was broken by the approach of what he could only believe was a German tank. It was headed straight for him and as it reached his trench it came to a halt with, believe it or not, one of its tracks resting directly above him. He was in mortal danger for if the tank had slewed in changing direction its track would have crushed him to death.

As it was he heard German voices; one of the crew alighted from the tank and the next thing Doug heard was Fritz answering the call of nature close by him. The German was chattering away quite unaware that a terrified British soldier was within inches of him. After he had done what he had to do, the soldier boarded the tank which started up, reversed and went on its way. No doubt Doug breathed a sigh of relief.

So did he really want to relive that terrifying moment? I tried to dissuade him from entering the wood. Not only did I not wish him to come to any harm, but I thought it would be exceedingly difficult if he did get injured and we had to call upon the local services to extricate him from that dangerous and forbidden place. But he went like a boy on an exploring venture. After about fifteen minutes he reappeared, holding something in his hand which resembled nothing in particular. It could have been a bit of war debris; personally I thought it bore resemblance to the type of knee pad used for horses. It was rotted and not worth keeping so we disposed of it. Doug said the wood was so overgrown that it was difficult to make progress through the matted undergrowth. He found it impossible to recognise anything of the 'Dorset Wood' where he nearly met his end.

Our next call was to Driel, location of another famous exploit of the 4th Dorsets, for it was here that they assisted the remnants of the 1st British Airborne Division to cross the Neder Rijn from Oosterbeek. During that engagement the regiment sustained, I believe, something in region of four hundred casualties. It was difficult on that peaceful sunny summer day to imagine the mayhem which had happened thirty five years previously. Of the ten thousand men of the airborne force only two thousand battle weary but unbowed veterans gained the safety of the southern shore of the river. Now we were watching people happily engaged in sunbathing at the water's edge and enjoying the thrill of water skiing. However, the events of those far off days are engraved for all time in the minds of the older people and in the history books of the town of Arnhem.

We visited Uden, a place never passed by, and took the opportunity of making the acquaintance of my correspondent friend of many years, Jan Heesen, and his wife Stine. We had been writing regularly since 1963. In response to a letter I had written to the Burgemeester of Uden Jan had replied, in his capacity of Secretary of the local branch of the Netherlands Oorlogsgraven Comite, that he would be pleased to place flowers on John's grave every November 21st, which was John's birthday. Jan has done this service for me regularly and without fail ever since, always including Stanley Matthews in the floral tributes. He told me only recently that he is so well known to the florist that she, knowing the reason for his custom, makes up a more than generous bouquet. We stayed with them overnight and they made us very welcome; so once again deep and lasting roots of friendship were established.

On reaching St Oedenrode we visited de Ollandseweg. What I believed to be, and in fact was, the old van Weert house had been modernised and was unrecognisable. Beside the house was a small petrol station with a single pump, above which was a sign saying 'TANK'. While having the car topped up I enquired of the young attendant whether the sign 'TANK' had any significance with the fact that a British tank had been knocked out directly opposite that station. He looked somewhat puzzled and said that 'TANK' meant petrol in Dutch and he had no knowledge of the event I had mentioned – so much for my ignorance. He spoke very good English so I outlined the story of the tank's destruction and mentioned the people from that house who had spoken to me in 1946 – two of the van Weert brothers. He then took Doug and me into the house and pointed to a large family portrait group to see if I could recognise anybody from many faces of his forebears, but I could not for it had been so long ago and my meeting with them brief. No doubt our visit to his petrol pump gave that Dutch lad a story to relate to his pals over his next lager. We noticed along de Ollandseweg that some of the trees still bore the scars left by the tracks of the tanks as they had trundled up that narrow road.

Visits were made to the van Uden family several times. By then the grandparents had died, but we were generously welcomed by everyone in that large family. This included Karl and Gerarda, Ben's sister, who lived near Anna who in the intervening years had moved from the family home in Eerschot to a small but pleasant cottage in the Goeveringslaan.

In 1979 we were delighted to be hosts to Jan and Stine for a week during their tour of England which began at Cambridge where their niece, I believe it was, was attending University. I sent detailed instructions to Jan to help him to reach Solihull without difficulty and now whenever I see him his face lights up as he recalls how he made that journey without once having to stop to ask a policeman the way, which I had suggested he do (tongue in cheek) if he got lost. At the age of eighty plus he is still a remarkably good driver and on a recent visit to his home he drove me for miles around his country to show me the sights.

Being involved with his local Uden library he was most interested to learn all about the new Solihull Library, which was purpose built and housed all the most modern library services. So I arranged for him to meet the Chief Librarian, who was most helpful. After coffee we were given a conducted tour to see the wide range of facilities on offer to the people of Solihull. The rest of the week was taken up with the usual tourist attractions of the region which always seem to give much pleasure to visitors. I do believe a picnic on a beautiful sunny day on the brow of Fish Hill overlooking Broadway and the Evesham valley stretching to the distant Malvern Hills was something of a new experience for them. A visit to Warwick Castle and Stratford, together with a little of the historical background to the events which have shaped the history of leafy Warwickshire added, I hope, to their pleasure.

A return visit to the Netherlands, at the invitation of Jan and Stine took place in 1980. We spent one week in St Oedenrode with Ben and Nettie and the second week with Jan and Stine in Uden. Jan made a point of taking us somewhere each day. He had arranged a very full programme which included the Carillon Museum in Asten, Hoendeloo, the Openlucht Museum at Arnhem, the beautiful ancient town of Heusden and a pleasurable visit to Nijmegen. Our last day was spent with them at a local nature park where we negotiated the duckboards with great care, not wanting to end up in the swamp with all the varied wildlife.

This was followed two years later with an organised tour from London to Nijmegen where Ivy, Douglas and I spent three days at the Hotel Erica – a popular place for British visitors with ex-service connections. Almost twenty years had elapsed since my visit with my mother in 1961. Here again we were teamed up with local people who had agreed to convey the 'pilgrims', as we were known, to the cemetery where their relative was buried. Wherever the graves were sited made no difference. Our host family were John and Truce Jacobs of Groesbeek. Following a pilgrimage to Uden Cemetery, where we were driven by John, we spent a delightful evening in their company at the hotel were also joined for dinner by Jan and Stine. Their attendance, at my request, had been agreed to by one Piet van Arnhem who was responsible for organising the 'do' and who, it was said, had been an active member of the Resistance in Arnhem during the war. On arriving at the dinner it was apparent that Jan and Piet were well known to each other – a small world indeed.

While at the hotel we decided to take a before dinner evening stroll around the district. While walking down the road in the direction of Nijmegen our English conversation attracted the attention of an elderly Dutch couple. Smiling, they approached us and enquired if we were British ex-servicemen. When Doug admitted to having been a member of the liberation army their joy was reflected in their faces. They eagerly shook our hands and told us how much they appreciated what Doug and other members had done for their country. They asked Doug if he was from the 7th Hampshires, for they had known several men from that battalion. Doug replied that he was a 'Dorset' but that he had fought alongside the 7th Hampshires from Normandy until the end of the war in Germany, they also being part of 130 Brigade of the 43rd Wessex Division. They went on to say how delighted they were to meet him and that they and many of their countrymen would never forget the British soldiers who had shown the Dutch people much kindness; sharing their food with them and giving their chocolate and sweet ration to the children. For us it was a very pleasant encounter and it was with reluctance that we had to refuse an invitation to their nearby home. Our organised tour did not, unfortunately, allow for such unscheduled excursions which was a great pity, for a chat with these delightful people would indeed have added to the pleasure of our tour. As it was, it reinforced our very high regard for the citizens of the Netherlands and confirmed the belief held by many ex-servicemen that the loss of so many young lives in that country had not been in vain.

It was during this tour that we visited the Reichwald War Cemetery near Cleve, which is the largest Commonwealth War Cemetery in Europe and contains many thousands of graves of men who lost their lives during the closing stages of World War II. Many of them died in the battle of the Reichwald Forest in February 1945, when the Germans fought with great ferocity to prevent the invasion of their homeland. Douglas had taken an active part in that battle and our visit to the cemetery was a poignant moment for him. Many of his Dorset comrades were buried there, but one had a special significance for him; the grave of Lance/Corporal Samways who had been his Section Commander. The story is that Doug was occupying a forward slit trench and was due to be relieved after his two hour stint. Samways came to relieve him from his position about two minutes before Doug's time was up; Doug got out of his trench and Samways got in and at that very moment a mortar bomb came over and hit the trench, killing Samways outright. Such are the fortunes of war. Whenever I go to the Reichwald Cemetery I make a point of placing a Legion poppy on his grave.

The cemetery is beautifully maintained. On the last occasion I went there with the Birmingham War Research Society after our visit to the Mohne and Eder dams (scene of the 'Dambusters' raid in May 1943) a service of remembrance took place. Ian Alexander played a lament on the pipes which drew in a few local Germans who, from a distance, appeared to be sharing silently in our tribute. As our coach drew away they stood there smiling, almost in sympathy, and they waved to us as the coach moved on, which I thought was something very meaningful. We returned their waves until they receded into the distance.

In Search of the Facts

THE YEAR 1989 SAW THE ARRIVAL THROUGH MY LETTER BOX ONE DAY in January of a quite unusual letter. It was from a man called Ad Hermens, a resident of the town of Geldrop near Eindhoven and the reasons for his writing to me have already been explained in the preface to this book.

I thought it quite remarkable that a Dutchman some forty five years after the end of the war would be interested to know about the soldiers, sailors and airmen who had lost their lives liberating his country. I acknowledged the fact that it was my brother he was enquiring about and also sent him a considerable amount of information gleaned from my visits to St Oedenrode in 1945 and 1946. I also enclosed photographs of John and of the tank in the ditch on de Ollandseweg.

I thought that would be the end of the matter, but I did not then know Ad Hermens and his insatiable desire to discover the truth about how our men met their deaths. Some weeks later another letter came from Ad to say that he had been discussing the incident in which John was killed with a colleague at the Philips factory where they both worked. This person was much aware of it and was acquainted with the van Weert family who would probably be able to tell him more.

This persuaded Ad to go to St Oedenrode and meet the van Weert brothers, Toon and Dorus. From the information they gave him he prepared a detailed sketch of what actually took place. They had witnessed much of it from the outbuilding to their house in which they had taken shelter from the battle raging around them. The details coincided to a large extent with what I had discovered earlier and also fitted in several unknown facts.

On approaching the junction of Rijsingen with de Ollandseweg, where the road begins to bear round to the right, the leading tank of 4 Troop, commanded by Lieutenant Cohen, was hit by fire from an anti-tank gun (75 or 88mm) of the 59th German Division. According to Dorus van Weert this was sited in a field to the left of the road, its aiming point obviously being on the bend of the approach road. This would be when any advancing tank would be most vulnerable and offer a wider target. The lead tank was hit twice, the shots being about twenty seconds apart. Nobody had any doubt that Matthews had died instantly What was again confirmed was that John had escaped from the tank and was shot by a German sniper some hundred yards away from the tank in the direction of St Oedenrode while attempting to get back to allied lines.

According to David Cohen, with whom I made contact in 1989, after the first shell hit the tank carried on forward out of control. He said he knew Matthews was dead and though wounded himself he had tried to lift John out, but he found this impossible to do. When the second shell hit he was blown off the tank onto the road. He was very surprised when I told him of the report of John's escape from the tank for he was convinced he was dead. In the confusion of battle it is difficult for anyone always to be certain about such things. Cohen added that he remembered that day quite vividly. He recalled feeling somewhat apprehensive about advancing up that narrow road, bounded as it was with trees and hedges which gave the advantage to the enemy. He also told me that he made several pleas to the US paratroopers of 'B' Company of the 502nd Parachute Infantry Regiment, who were occupying fox holes along the roadside, to accompany him to give support in the event of running into the enemy. This they had refused to do; no doubt they had their orders to stay put.

So the troop of two tanks proceeded towards Olland, the next village, without infantry support. While advancing Lieutenant Cohen sent several shots from his seventeen pounder gun into the windmill situated on the left front of the line of advance. He felt it might be in use as a German observation post and this assumption was correct. As a result of his shelling the mill was so badly damaged that it had to be demolished after the war; today there is no trace of it and a modern house occupies the site. The following tank of the troop also suffered a hit from the German anti-tank gun and in the face of such accurate fire it withdrew from the action. Lieutenant Cohen and the Wireless Operator, whose name is unknown to me, reached allied lines where Lieutenant Cohen was hospitalised suffering from wounds and burns. He did not return to the Regiment until December 1944.

A very graphic account of the events of that afternoon was sent to me recently by my friend Henri van Weert, in the form of a newspaper article which had appeared in the local newspaper *Midden Brabant* on September 18th 1985. This was a story related by one Mr Wim van Keulen, who as a twelve year old refugee from Heelen had come to live in hiding in St Oedenrode with his family. They were given shelter with the family of Janus van der Meijden whose farm was next to that of the van Weert family on de Ollandseweg.

Wim van Keulen recalled quite vividly, and in great detail, the events which took place on September 17th 1944 and how he witnessed the great air armada approaching in the direction of Arnhem, the destruction of allied planes and the awe inspiring advance of 30 Corps troops along 'The Corridor'. But even more vivid was his account of the activities of the German troops of the 59th Division who had advanced from Boxtel with the intention of cutting the vital axis route. Along this were streaming long columns of armour and support vehicles heading for the beleaguered airborne troops some fifty miles distant. The van der Meijden farm was in the middle of the German lines and he was able to observe the setting up of defensive positions when faced with an allied attack from the direction of St Oedenrode. They were heavily shelled by allied gunfire, situated in Nijnsel, which was directed at the German positions. The main part of the story is that relating to the destruction of the leading tank of 4 troop. He wrote:-

> Opposite the van der Meijden farm a German anti-tank gun was in position.
>
> In the afternoon of the 21 September, this gun was fired, followed immediately by a loud cheering which we could hear in the cellar. It appeared that from the direction of the village along de Ollandseweg in the direction of Olland, a formation of two Sherman tanks drove in our direction. At a bend in the road near a farm a tank had been hit by this German gun. This explained the triumphant shouting of the Germans.
>
> Some members of its crew tried to escape and were shot down by the Germans. The other tank must have turned back in the direction of the village.
>
> The tank that was hit exploded from the inside and was burnt out. That evening a part of de Ollandseweg showed a bizarre scene, a burning hay stack and a blazing tank.

Above: My first meeting with Ad Hermans in 1991 - well shot, Henri!

Above: Inspecting a part of the tank's armour plate in Toon's workshop

Left: With Toon and Dorus van Weert at the spot where Dorus found John

Above: Ad, Moppie and Pia at their home in Geldrop, 1993

Above: Toon, Anneke, Henri, Dorus and Mien in the garden at their home in de Ollandesweg in May 1993

Above: Ties, whose home is directly behind the union flag, standing with the floral tributes laid by the various local authorities in Uden on the evening of May 4th 1993, following the Commemoration service in Uden church

Above: John and Stan's graves, with the childrens' roses

Above: From left to right are – Jeanny Kleijne, H Vonk, Pia and Ad Hermens, Major Bob Lockwood, Anneke and Toon van Weert, Louis Kleijne, Dorus and Henri van Weert.

Above: Piper Ian Alexander entertaining 'de Dorsvlegels' at our AC Hotel Zevenum – a magical evening

Above: The British Legion Standard party at Uden Cemetery in May 1994 (the graves of John and Stan are in the foreground)

Left: Two very nice fellows, Frank Lea and Fred Williams – both holders of the Military Medal. This was taken in 1989; sadly, Frank died a few months later

Right: Jan and Stine Heesen in the grounds of Het Loo Palace – they always have a bed available for me at St Annastraat and on November 21st each year Jan places flowers on John's grave

Above: Receiving one of the fifty one roses

Above: Children of the Kienehoefschool at the ceremony
held in St Martins Churchyard in 1993

Left: Louis at work carving the plinth

Right: The bronze plaque

Above: Family representatives at the memorial – sons Moayad, John and self – with Ad Hermens and Dutch children looking on

Left: Dorus van Weert, who buried John, laying the wreath of poppies

Above: The author with Louis Kleijne and son John plus a few of the multitude who attended the memorial ceremony

For that family the battle continued unabated for several days during which time they noted where the German positions were located. The van der Meijden farm, in which they were still sheltering, was fortified by the Germans. But eventually it was also set on fire and on the orders of the SS they left the cellar in which they had sheltered and fled under intense fire to the comparative safety of a nearby ditch. After several attempts and despite heavy shell and machine gun fire from both sides, they were eventually allowed to cross the front line – with the help of a German machine gunner who turned a blind eye. They managed to reach the area of Kienehoef where they were taken to the local American commander to whom they gave information about the disposition of the German gun and mortar sites and the observation post situated in the windmill.

Wim van Keulen and his family found temporary accommodation in St Oedenrode; for the most part this was underground. After several days, and once the German front had been pushed back to near the transformer station of de Ollandseweg, the van der Meijden family returned to their home via Cathalijnepad (which was strewn with dead soldiers) to find their farm completely destroyed. The van Keulen family went to the home of one van Kuyk where they made preparations to return to their home in Heelen which had already been liberated. They left St Oedenrode on October 8th 1944.

Another interesting factor in this story came to light only recently, during the last reunion meeting of the 44th RTR in Bristol in November 1993 (I have had the privilege of attending those reunions for the past four years).

Ex Corporal Doug Brown, MM, introduced himself to me and asked if I was Jackie's brother. He then went on to relate that he had earlier in the campaign been the commander of that tank and all those men, including Jack, were his crew. They had been together during most of the fierce fighting in North West Europe.

Unfortunately, he had been evacuated to hospital with malaria some time prior to 'Market Garden' and command of his tank had been assumed by Lieutenant Cohen for that particular operation. He said it was a great shock to him when he returned to the Regiment just two days after two of his crew members had been killed. He added that it was very bad luck for they had survived many a battle together since landing in Normandy in June.

A final revealing contribution which perhaps explains why Lieutenant Cohen advanced without paratroop support was sent to me by Henri van Weert as an extract from the book *Eindol Maas* by Jack Didden and Maarten Swarts, an account entitled 'Clean Up Around St Oedenrode'. In this it is stated that because of a misunderstanding (by whom it is not made clear) in the thrusts by the troops of 'C' Squadron towards Olland and Schijndel, the tanks advanced too far ahead and the lead tanks of both troops were put out of action. The following tanks were also hit and had to withdraw. Bad communication between the British and the Americans was admitted and on the evening of September 21st the Commander of 'C' Squadron (Major 'Teddy' Foster) ordered his crews to hold their positions in accordance with the instructions given by the American Colonel Cassidy earlier in the day. At 8pm the British tank crews noticed to their astonishment that the US paratroopers were withdrawing to St Oedenrode. When Major Foster demanded an explanation for this he was informed by the paratroopers that Colonel Cassidy had that afternoon given them permission to withdraw, but he had failed to inform his British colleagues.

General Taylor, Commander of 101 Division, to achieve his mission to hold and defend the vital 'Corridor' with the forces available to him, compared this operation with the defence of the railroads in the developing post Civil War United States against raids by the marauding Indians, where judgement had to be made as to the best method of discouraging and preventing such attacks. This, apparently, had been to locate forces along the railroad at key points with the ability to move rapidly to meet hostile incursions – shades of British Imperial defence policy on the North West Frontier of India. Defence of 'The Corridor' was, in his view, a similar situation and while engaging in normal patrolling it was not intended that the bulk of his force should deploy widely to seek out the enemy and become involved in bloody and costly engagements which could detract from the main object of his task which was to keep the road open for 30 Corps troops. Therefore, a fine balance had to be struck to meet the rapidly changing situation following upon the Germans' unexpected and aggressive reaction to the airborne invasion. This may account for the US paratroopers remaining in their slit trenches along de Ollandseweg and maybe waiting, according to orders, for any sign of the enemy approaching from the direction of Olland. Maybe the British forces acting in support of the Americans were not privy to that policy. The involvement of both in this joint action had no doubt, like the rest of 'Market Garden', ocurred with little pre-planning and it was to be expected that misunderstandings would occur – war is a confusing and complex business and such things are bound to happen. This whole operation had more than its full share of errors, which were compounded by the lack of time for preparation.

Accounts about 'Market Garden' reveal that the US paratroopers were aggressive and doughty warriors and the 82nd Airborne Division earned immortal fame consequent upon the gallant action of the 504 Regiment for their magnificent achievement in forcing the crossing of Waal on September 20th. This was undertaken in fragile paddle-powered canvas boats in the face of fierce and sustained opposition from the Germans entrenched on the northern bank of the river. Despite heavy losses in both men and boats, the paratroopers attacked the Germans with great determination and put the enemy to flight, but at considerable cost to themselves.

It is interesting to relate that in addition to the support of the 44th RTR the Americans enlisted the help of one Sergeant McCrory of the Irish Guards, whose tank had earlier been disabled in the St Oedenrode area. Being unable to go forward with the main advance of the Guards Armoured Division, he had offered his help to the Americans. His tank could only move very slowly but despite this McCrory did sterling work with the US forces on those two crucial days, which included the destruction of a battery of three 20mm guns and an 88mm gun. He was obviously a very competent and resourceful NCO and for his achievements in support of the paratroopers he was awarded the American Silver Star.

That concludes the story of what was a minor engagement in the much larger battle taking place to relieve the gallant but beleaguered airborne troops at Arnhem. That story is an epic in itself and has been recounted in several excellent historical works on 'Market Garden'. The 44th RTR played a very significant role and was referred to in the book *The Devil's Birthday* by Geoffrey Powell as 'the ubiquitous 44th RTR'. This was but a repetition of what they had been doing constantly since they first went to North Africa in an active role some three years previously.

Bravery, courage and endurance was exhibited during those crucial days by those engaged in the battle, whether American, British, Polish or German. The 'Butcher's Bill' was tremendous. Of the ten thousand British and Polish airborne forces who landed in the Arnhem area over 6500 finished up in POW camps in Germany, 1700 of them being wounded. The cemetery at Oosterbeek is the final resting place for 1747 men, the majority, about 1500, being airborne casualties. The presence there of two very young lads, the Gronert twins – No 5511523 Private Thomas Gronert and 5511524 Private Claude Gronert – is a poignant testimony to the tragedy and heartbreak 'Market Garden' brought to many a British home that Autumn in 1944. Only 2000 airborne troops escaped across the Neder Rijn to fight another day.

For the US airborne forces the cost was a total in excess of 3800 casualties, while the British ground troops lost over 5000 and aircrew about 700, with a loss of 261 aircraft destroyed and 1453 damaged. One must not forget the Dutch people themselves who suffered many deaths and paid heavily indeed for that operation. In addition to the casualties in lives and extensive damage to property, the Germans inflicted severe reprisals against them in the town of Arnhem and surrounding areas for the willing aid they had courageously given to the allied forces. German losses in 'Market Garden' amounted to up to ten thousand men.

It was a high price indeed for an operation which, as research reveals, was conceived in haste and with a lack of in-depth planning. There are several fundamental reasons for its failure, but the one crucial error was to have ignored hard intelligence of the presence of German armour in the Arnhem area. These were the remnants of two German Armoured Divisions who were refitting after the hammering they had received in the earlier battles in France. Though depleted, they had sufficient tanks and self-propelled guns to make their presence a decisive factor in determining the outcome of the battle.

As an illumination on the help given to allied troops by the Dutch, and on my post-war personal experience too, the following is an extract from the book *Prisoner of the Reich*, by David Rolf, about British prisoners in German hands during 1939 to 1945 and relates to a Private Low who was captured at the time of Dunkirk and was being marched through France and the low countries en route to a camp in Germany:

> A Private Low, trudging through three defeated countries, observed sharp differences between them:
>
> French people offering food received a German rifle butt for their pains – such is war.
>
> Crossing into Belgium was frightening – there seemed to be no civilians, everyone was keeping to their houses.
>
> Holland gave us a boost – the end of the journey on foot and people impervious to the German rifles giving us loaves, sausages, anything they could get past the guards to us – wonderful people.

The 44th RTR saw further action in the Netherlands during the winter of 1944-45, with forays into Belgium. This was followed by the breaching of the supposedly impregnable Seigfried Line and the Rhine Crossing, when the 44th had the distinction of being the first tanks to cross that river, in the vicinity of Xanten. The tanks were waterproofed, fitted with a skirt, and after only ten days training were floated across the river like bath tubs, steered by a tiller and driven by a small propeller geared to the tank's engine. This was a very hazardous undertaking but was achieved successfully and with few casualties. Finally, as the war drew to its close the 44th continued to advance into Germany being engaged continuously against a desperate and determined enemy, including pockets of fanatical Nazi resistance, until they reached the northern city of Bremen where they fired their last shot in anger. They were among the original 'Desert Rats' and the Regiment lost a total of 231 officers and men who lie in graves stretching from North Africa to Germany. Their names are recorded in perpetuity on the Regimental memorial plaque in the TAVR Centre in Whiteladies Road, Bristol.

As well as many Mentions in Dispatches, a total of fifty five gallantry awards were made for outstanding acts of heroism as follows:

> Five Distinguished Service Orders
> One Order of the Crown and Croix De Guerre (Belgium)
> Fifteen Military Crosses plus one bar
> One Distinguished Service Cross (USA)
> Three Distinguished Conduct Medals
> One British Empire Medal
> Twenty Six Military Medals plus one bar
> One Croix De Guerre (France)

In my endeavour to contact Lieutenant Cohen I was helped initially by Ron Allen, that tireless and long serving Secretary of the 44th RTR Old Comrades Association, who sadly died in November 1993 shortly prior to what was to be the last annual reunion. Ron very kindly put me in touch with ex Lieutenant Fred Williams, MM, of Ashford, Kent who (Ron said) was an old friend of David Cohen. They had both served with the 6th RTR and were commissioned together in Egypt in 1943. After being commissioned their ways parted until they met up again in the 44th RTR in Normandy. As a result of the information Fred Williams gave me I was able, eventually, to contact David Cohen with whom I exchanged several letters and spoke on the telephone. It was then that I learned of his recollections, though misted with time, of the events of September 21st 1944.

Ron Allen had kindly invited me to the 1989 reunion and when Fred Williams learned of this he asked me to join him as his guest, which I thought a very friendly gesture on his part. So on the weekend of November 10th and 11th we met at the Oakfield Hotel. Fred proved to be a very friendly and sincere man and we got on well from the outset. Since that first meeting we have joined each other at every subsequent reunion. I must say, I found everyone in Bristol very chummy and it surprised me that so many ex-members of the Regiment still regularly attended such reunions after forty odd years. Surprisingly, two of them travelled every year from as far away as Australia and New Zealand to be with their old comrades. This, surely, was an indication of the strong esprit-de-corps which must always have existed in the Regiment.

I had not gone to Bristol with the intention of looking for people who had known John, but quite by chance on that first visit Ron Allen introduced me to Frank Lea, MM, of York – the very same Frank Lea whose exploits in the Sicily campaign have been mentioned earlier in this book and which won him a well deserved Military Medal. When Ron mentioned my name by way of introduction Frank was visibly surprised to meet me. It was some moments before he recovered from his initial shock and with an air of almost disbelief he then asked 'Are you really Jackie's brother?' When I replied that I was he seemed to be struck dumb – he had to sit down to recover himself and I could see tears welling in his eyes. It took him some minutes and the aid of a double whisky to regain his senses and he then surprised me by saying that he had been trying to trace me for some time. He put his hand in his pocket and took out two photographs which were of the graves of John and Stan in Uden cemetery. He said he had obtained these through the office of a Mr Jeggerins of Nuenen who, in 1988, had attended the 44th RTR reunion.

Frank said John's death had affected him greatly because they had seen so much action together since John had joined the Regiment in Africa. He ended with the words 'George, I thought a lot of young Jackie, he was a smashing lad and while I am alive he will never be forgotten'. I was too moved by these words to say very much, especially as they came from someone who had known John so many years ago. Here he was, an intrepid old soldier as tough as they make them, with two photographs in his pocket and exhibiting such a depth of feeling for my brother that made me feel very humble.

As with Fred Williams, my relationship with Frank Lea became friendship overnight. Both were men of calibre and sincerity and I found it indeed a wonderful experience to be among the old soldiers of the 44th, all of whom appeared to have grown old gracefully. It did not take much imagination to realise what the Regiment had meant to them. There were quite a few characters among them such as Tosh Peedell, formerly of 'A' Squadron, and Fred Williams, former driver (usually accompanied by his sons and grandson). I felt at home among them and was treated with much kindness by everyone.

After that meeting, Frank wrote me the following letter:

York, 14/11/1989

Dear George

Many thanks for your letter just received. I'm in the middle of letter writing so I'll answer straight away.

I'm very glad we met as its been in my mind for about a year to trace the next of kin of Jackie and Stan. However, fate solved the problem for me by you turning up. The way I obtained the photos is rather strange as in February 1987 I received a letter from Jan Jeggerins, of Nuenen, Holland, asking for information concerning the 44th's actions during 'Market Garden' in September 1944, as he was writing a book on the liberation of North Brabant, and particularly his village of Nuenen, where two of our men were killed (Cpl. Stothard and Tpr. Nichols). The lady who was with me at Bristol last weekend was Ralph Stothard's widow. Jan traced her after forty three years and indirectly this was how we met, through him.

Subsequently I photographed the relevant chapter of our 44th *History*, together with the Roll of Honour of the lads killed in Holland during September, 1944. He sent me the photo of Jackie's grave a little later, as Uden is not far from Nuenen.

Also last year he came to the reunion at Bristol and made a wonderful speech of thanks for our war time efforts. The lads rose and cheered him, which had never happened before to any speaker. But this year he has had to cancel his intended visit as his old mother is very ill, she's ninety one. Which reminds me to ask if you will be there next year, 1990, and you and I will meet again, if not before should you be in the York area.

To return to Jackie, he was in 5 Troop in Normandy but not in my crew or he was at one time the CO's gunner in HQ Troop (Major Teddy Foster). Stan was my driver at one time but eventually they both went into 4 Troop on Lt. David Cohen's tank for the 'Market Garden' job. Jackie was a real nice lad and never gave any trouble at all, dead steady on the job and no 'ramming around' in the back areas like certain blokes I could name. Stan was different, he was in fact the more dominant of the two and had been known to argue the toss occasionally, but a good driver nevertheless. I was greatly upset when they were killed and swore revenge on the whole ruddy world as well as on the German army.

George, I want you to keep the photostat of the Chapter 24 of our *History*, also the Roll of Honour where I've marked all the lads killed in Holland.

Fortunately nobody was ever killed in my turret when I was commanding; but on one occasion in Holland, just north of Veghel I was knocked out after my gunner had KO'd a Panther. There were two there nearby and they got me, but none of my crew were hurt even though my driver was badly shocked and was not fit for weeks afterwards.

That's enough lamp swinging for today. One thing for sure I'll never forget the lads, especially those two, they were such good mates. RIP.

I'll sign off now George so keep in touch and knock on my door anytime. Cherrio for now old son.

Yours, Frank

There followed the roll of 5 Troop who appeared on a photograph in Frank's album, which was taken in Normandy soon after landing in June 1944. Regrettably I do not have a copy of that historical photograph. They were:

Lance/Corporal Jack Lafford (killed in action June 29th 1944)
Trooper Des Troth
Trooper Arthur Brock (killed in action November 29th 1944)
Trooper Jim Whiting
Trooper Tom Darbyshire
Trooper Bill 'Jack' Kerr
Corporal Frank Lea
Trooper Jock Fraser
Trooper Chas Lucas
Trooper Stan Matthews (killed in action September 21st 1944)
Trooper Bomb Harris
Trooper Fred Ford
Lance/Corporal Boogie Lawrence
Trooper Rene Houston
Trooper Jackie Thorogood (killed in action September 21st 1944)

During our several telephone conversations Frank expressed a desire to go to the Netherlands, but he said he was a little concerned about travelling alone as his 'ticker' was not too good. I therefore suggested we make a trip together, as I knew the country quite well and had many friends in the 'Market Garden' area, which he particularly wanted to see again.

Unfortunately, and to the great sorrow of myself and many of his mates in the 44th, Frank died suddenly of a heart attack on March 17th 1990, just four short months after we had first met. Although I had known him only briefly I felt I had lost an old friend. He was the sort of man one could warm to quite easily and I had anticipated seeing a lot of him. It was odd also to think that for over forty years my family had been visiting the

York area regularly, where an old army pal of mine lived. I might well have met Frank without realising who he was. To you too, Frank, RIP.

At the Bristol reunions the Sunday morning remembrance service was always a very special occasion. One often heard some of the men speaking with deep feeling about the pals they had lost in some far off battlefield and all shared in a common tribute to them. I felt privileged to be among them.

Alas, it was decided by the Old Comrades Association for several reasons, including declining numbers, that the time had come to bring to a close the annual reunions which had covered almost half a century. It was with some regret that I attended the final meeting on November 13th 1993. For many, whose comradeship had begun way back in the dark and uncertain days of September 1939, it must have been a very sad moment to bid one another a final farewell. In his closing paragraph of the report of the 48th and final meeting of the Association, Bill Green wrote:

> Only a great Regiment could have maintained such solid support over nearly half a century. Everyone who served, however fleetingly, within its ranks was touched by its quality and warmth, and in return left a bit of themselves, and their service behind, and I am virtually certain that the 44th will still be the main topic of conversation as long as there remain but a handful of us left around a table in some saloon bar in the years ahead. God bless you all.

Unlike many of the old established and 'fashionable' regiments, many of which, sadly, have long been disbanded, the 44th had no individual museum in which to record their exploits. However, the Regimental scrapbook containing a host of historical facts, together with the flag which accompanied them into their first action in North Africa, has been deposited in the Tank Museum, Bovington, along with other 44th memorabilia and the now rare *History of the 44th Royal Tank Regiment 1939-45*. So at least an historical record will always be available as a testimony to the quality and fighting spirit of the 'ubiquitous' 44th.

In May 1991 my wife and I travelled to Arnhem with the Birmingham War Research Society. This is based in King's Norton and is run jointly by two tireless gentlemen, both Jocks; Alex Bullock and Ian Alexander. They run an excellent service to the Continent conveying relatives and ex-servicemen to a wide range of historical battle sites in France, Belgium, the Netherlands and Germany. Their itinerary includes such places as the Normandy Beaches, the Somme, Dunkirk, Arnhem, the Reichwald, Colditz and the Mohn and Eder Dams. They assist relatives in tracing the graves of soldiers, sailors or airmen whose resting place or memorial is unknown to the family. Often they convey relatives to a graveside not visited in seventy or more years. They work on a non profit making basis and make generous donations to the Commonwealth War Graves Commission, the Earl Haig Poppy Fund, The Royal British Legion and various other service related charities. To reach a particular cemetery they will often travel many miles off route; their trips usually cover a long weekend from late on Thursday evening until the return on the following Monday.

Following lengthy and regular correspondence with Ad Hermens, the avid researcher from Geldrop, I had a wish to meet with both him and members of the van Weert family. I thought it would be a good idea if we all met in St Oedenrode. To this end I proposed to take a day off from the official coach tour, which was to include visits to the Airborne Cemetery at Oosterbeek, the dropping zones and museums, which I had done before. Instead, I would make my own way to St Oedenrode. With the help of a very cooperative and efficient receptionist at the West End Hotel, who produced for me a printed schedule of train timetables, I set off by taxi for Arnhem railway station. Arriving very speedily at St Hertogenbosch I then took the local bus and reached St Oedenrode by about 11am, the time I had suggested I might arrive.

The bus dropped me off at the junction with de Ollandseweg, but as with my visit ten years earlier I had no idea where I was; so much building had taken place that it was like being in a completely new town. With an enquiry to a Dutch lady who was busily sweeping her drive, I was pointed in the direction for Olland. Stepping out at a good pace, after about twenty minutes I saw a group of four men standing on the left hand side of the road, obviously waiting for me. It was quite a momentous occasion. Not only was this my first meeting with Ad Hermens, but it was through his efforts that this reunion with the van Weert brothers, Dorus and Toon, was taking place after forty five years.

They, like me, had been young men in 1946 so it was not at all strange that we failed to recognise one another; and in any case our meeting in 1946 had been brief. The fourth man in the group was introduced to me as Henri van Weert, son of Toon, who has since become a regular and prolific correspondent. This time there was to be no language barrier for both Ad Hermens and Henri van Weert have an excellent command of the English language. We went to the home of Toon where I was introduced to his wife, Anneke; to Pia, Ad's companion; and to Mien, the wife of Dorus, who proved later to be something of a poet. In that congenial company over coffee and cakes we conversed about many things. Henri proved to be a charming young man, assisting with interpreting and the taking of many photographs, for my coming seemed to be regarded as an important visit. During the course of the morning Toon produced an entrenching tool which he said he had recovered from inside the tank and which he now offered to me as another memento. Ad also presented me with a pair of antique Dutch children's clogs, on the insides of which he had inscribed the names of John and Stan, their regiment and the date of my visit. Later, on a tour of Toon's workshop, he showed me a large piece of armour plate which had been purloined when the tank was cut up for scrap in 1946.

Lunch was provided by the charming Anneke, who smilingly chattered away in Dutch as she dispensed more coffee. Despite the reason for my being in their company it was not a dull or depressing meeting, for who could be downhearted among those friendly folk? In fact, I think we were all very pleased to meet one another and a very convivial atmosphere prevailed.

After lunch it was suggested that we go to the actual spot where John's body was found. This was about 150 yards beyond the van Weert home at Rijsingen in the direction of Olland, on the opposite side of the road, directly in front of a cottage. It was a sad moment for me to be reminded where Dorus had found him, and then to see again the site in the adjoining field where he had buried him.

We all then walked together for about a hundred or more yards further up the road to the place where the tank came to rest. The site now bears no resemblance to my earlier memory of it; the road has been widened and a cycle path built. The van Weert home, which appears in the background of the picture of the tank, had yet again been remodernised beyond all recognition. In fact, I asked what had happened to the old house and was told it was still the same house but the exterior had been completely refurbished. The modernisation of old property is a very widespread practice in the Netherlands today for one seldom sees any ramshackle old buildings. I could only surmise that they must be very well-to-do. Neat and tidy is the Dutch way, and we could learn a lot from them.

A few more yards up the road brought us to the home of

Dorus and his wife Mien. No sooner had we sat ourselves down on the rear patio than coffee and cakes were served by Mien; the fact that we had been eating lunch only an hour or so earlier was ignored – an excellent Dutch custom!

Dorus spoke about the heavy fighting which had taken place on that stretch of the road and which continued for many days after September 21st. They were right in the middle of it as the German line of defence was situated almost where we were then sitting. He added that many Germans had been killed and pointed out a ditch behind his house where two German snipers were positioned to fire on the advancing allied forces whose task it was to prevent the Germans reaching and cutting the vital 'Corridor'. He said he had managed to get a message through to the US paratroopers, one of whom tossed a grenade into the German trench, killing both occupants. I was also told that the large farmhouse next to Toon's home in Rijsingen had been used as a field dressing station by the British who had tended the wounded of both sides.

Dorus too had a souvenir from the tank. He went to his workshop and came out with a large sledgehammer which he said had been a very useful tool on his farm. It was difficult, sitting drinking coffee in that peaceful place on that sunny Spring afternoon, with everyone reminiscing about those events of long ago, to imagine that forty seven years previously such horrors took place there. So many young men from both sides had lost their lives through the evil of one man, Adolf Hitler, bringing so much sorrow and grief to their loved ones.

On taking my leave from those hospitable people, Ad – accompanied by Pia, who was shortly to become his wife – kindly took me Uden to the house of my long-standing friends Jan and Stine Heesen, who were expecting me. It was ten years since we had met at the Hotel Erica in Nijmegen but, as always, our reunion was warm and friendly and it was an opportunity to swap family news. I stayed with them for two short hours, during which time I again had to partake of coffee and cakes. They then took me by car to Oss, the nearest railway station, where I caught a train back to Arnhem. It had been a very busy but memorable day which I felt had been more than worthwhile; thanks to Ad I had made and cemented several new friendships. I returned to the hotel laden with gifts, for I had also collected chocolates and home produced honey from Jan and Stine to add to those gifts received in St Oedenrode.

The culmination of our visit to the Netherlands was the holding of a brief memorial service at Uden cemetery. This had been arranged by Ian and Alex to take place on the Monday morning of our return journey home and was attended by Jan and Stine and Ties Verstegen.

Ties Verstegen, whose home is directly opposite the cemetery, has unofficially adopted it and provides many services for relatives of the soldiers and airmen buried there. He arranges for flowers to be laid on graves at certain times in accordance with the wishes of relatives, takes photographs of graves on request and assists in a variety of ways. Much of the cost comes from his own pocket. In conjunction with two colleagues, P Hannen and A Verbakel, he formed the Foundation Uden War Cemetery several years ago. Its aim is to commemorate every year those who gave their lives in liberating the Netherlands in World War II. These men, together with their wives, arrange for relatives to go to Uden in May each year to join with the local community in celebrating their liberation in May 1945. The British visitors are accommodated free of charge in Dutch homes. They are wined and dined and are entertained with visits to local places of interest, such as Arnhem. The visit culminates with a commemoration service in the nearby church which is followed by a wreath-laying ceremony in the cemetery. I have written more about this in a later chapter.

On this day in 1991 our own impromptu service with all the coach party present, together with out Dutch friends, was very special for me. Ian played a lament on his pipes which, in this quiet Dutch town, immediately attracted several of the local populace who must have wondered what was happening – after all, it isn't often one sees a lone Scots piper in all his regalia piping so far away from his native shores.

It was appropriate, too, that Jan was present for he had been associated with the cemetery since 1943 when it was first opened for the burial of allied war dead. On arrival at the cemetery I noticed that fresh flowers had been placed on John's and Stan's graves, a kindly gesture of Jan's which he always makes if he knows I am coming to Uden. Jan was asked to read out Laurence Binyon's immortal words:

> *They shall not grow old, as we who are left grow old:*
> *Age shall not weary them, nor the years condemn.*
> *At the going down of the sun and in the morning*
> *We will remember them.*

Yes, it was a very special day and it was particularly pleasing to learn that my poem on Uden cemetery (reproduced at the front of this book) had been translated into Dutch and read out at the commemoration service some days previously. It soon transpired that I was not the only person moved to poetry. Shortly after returning to England I was sent a beautiful poem by Mien van Weert, dedicated to John, which is reproduced on the opposite page.

John

U was nog jong en mooi
Het leven was voor U nog een droom
Gij moest ver weg
Van huis en haard
U deed uw plicht
Als een soldaat
Gij voaht voor ons bestaan
Al bent U van ons heen gegaan
In ons hardt
Blijf gij geschreven staan

This translates into English as:

You were so young and handsome
Life was still a dream for you
You had to go far away
Leaving hearth and home
You were doing your duty
As a soldier
You fought for our survival
Although you have passed away
Your name stays within our hearts

Commemoration Days In Noord Brabant

IN 1993 I ACCEPTED AN INVITATION FROM THE FOUNDATION UDEN War Cemetery to join with the people of Uden at their Commemoration Service on May 4th.

Some months earlier I had received a letter from Louis Kleijne, Headmaster of the Kienehoefschool in St Oedenrode, informing me that it was the practice at this school each year to undertake a project with the senior pupils about World War II. The purpose of this was to remind the children about the liberation of their country, the horrors of war and the unhappiness it brings to families, the value of freedom and the need to guard against oppression. He stressed that its aim was to make the children aware of the sacrifices made by the men of the allied forces who lost their lives during the war and in particular those who died in the Autumn of 1944 during the liberation of St Oedenrode.

He added that it had come to his notice through Ties Verstegen, during a visit to Uden Cemetery, that my brother John had been killed on de Ollandseweg not far from his school and also that I, John's brother, would be coming to the

Netherlands for the Commemoration service. He asked whether I would be willing during my time there to go to the school and speak to the children and answer questions about my family during the war, but more especially about my brother. Despite some initial misgivings at the prospect of facing some fifty children in a foreign, though no doubt friendly, school and knowing little or no Dutch with which to communicate, I accepted the invitation.

I referred Louis Kleijne to Ad Hermens in Geldrop, who had prepared quite a remarkable framed display of information about John which he had shown at his annual exhibition of World War II artifacts at a local bank in Geldrop. I felt sure he would gladly make it available to the school. In addition, I sent several photographs and documents to assist the school with their project.

Having accepted the invitation I began to think it was high time for me to make some effort to learn some basic Dutch. For nigh on fifty years I had selfishly relied upon the ability of the Dutch people, especially those of the younger generation, to speak English. Henri van Weert, for example, is equally fluent in English, German and French, which I find remarkable. So, thinking it might be helpful to show at least some effort to speak or understand a few words, I purchased a Hugo Cassette Language Course – *Dutch in Three Months*. Many long hours were spent during the winter months of 1992-93 trying to assimilate something of the Dutch tongue. It was not easy, particularly having nobody with whom to practice conversation or to consult in those less well understood areas.

The Kienehoefschool had already established close links with the South Yorkshire Market Garden Veterans Association, who go to the school whenever they visit the Netherlands. The children are also in correspondence with children of Wheatley Hills Middle School in Doncaster. Links were strengthened with that school following a visit to Yorkshire by Louis Kleijne and his wife Jeanny, with two other Dutch representatives, at the end of May 1993. On that occasion Louis Kleijne met a Mrs Abbie Etherington, the widow of one of the English soldiers – a Sergeant George Dry, of the East Riding Yeomanry, who was killed just outside St Oedenrode in October 1944. His grave, along with those of twenty two other British servicemen who lie in the local churchyard, is regularly tended by staff and pupils of the school. Mrs Etherington was presented with gifts, which included a framed photograph of the grave and a video tape of the service which had taken place in the churchyard on May 4th.

My invitation to the school was for May 4th. This clashed with my planned arrangements, for originally I had agreed to be in Uden from May 1st-4th and to go to St Oedenrode and Geldrop later. As the school could not change their arrangements because of holiday closure, with the ready agreement of my friends I changed the schedule around completely. Happily, in the event, everything went as smoothly as clockwork. Nevertheless, the planned programme for Tuesday May 4th was a full one and had to be carefully organised so that my various commitments were not compromised.

My journey to the Netherlands began at 7.15am on April 29th, when my good friend Larry Allcott called to convey me by car to Birmingham Airport for my flight to Eindhoven. The aeroplane was a small eighteen seater carrying mainly businessmen. I seemed to be the only one with a surfeit of luggage for the majority of passengers carried just a briefcase or at most a holdall. I was loaded with a medium suitcase plus two large parcels containing various gifts for my many Dutch friends. The flight to Eindhoven was uneventful, though we were offered a breakfast of sorts, and refreshments. The crew were Dutch and the stewardess spoke English with not the slightest trace of an accent. We touched down at about 10.45am and I was met at the airport by Ad and Pia. Ad had mounted himself on the airport roof to video my arrival; this was the beginning of a recording of my four days in Geldrop and St Oedenrode.

My correspondence with Ad over the intervening two years had been frequent and lengthy so we felt like old friends meeting again. On the way to Geldrop, which is quite near to Eindhoven, we stopped for coffee and cakes at the home of their close friends, Yo and Wim van Dongen in Frederick Laan. There I was given a guided tour of Wim's museum which is located in his garden shed and which contains all manner of bits and pieces of the debris of war; guns, helmets, shell cases and the like. Where do they find it? Yo, the lady of the house, another English speaker, explained their interest in British veterans and their close link with the Irish Guards, whose regimental plaque was proudly displayed on the wall in the lounge. The Irish Guards had led the advance of the Guards Armoured Division up 'The Corridor'. Yo explained that their affection for British ex-servicemen began way back in 1944 when, as a child, she was given some sweets by a British soldier. She could not remember having had sweets before and that was a marvellous and unforgettable moment for her. They were due to have a veteran of the Irish Guards and his wife to stay with them the following week.

On reaching the home of Ad in Papenvoort in neighbouring Geldrop I was introduced to Moppie, Pia's eighty nine year old mother; who was a very sweet lady, but very frail. We got on famously and I teased her quite a lot, which she seemed to enjoy. One could see that she doted on Ad, her son-in-law, who showed her much affection and concern. The Hermens' home was a warm and welcoming place, full of treasures and antiques of many and varying kinds; wherever one looked one saw something not spotted before. I had never before been in such a house. My bedroom alone would be child's paradise, being full of toys and bric a brac, pictures, dolls and teddy bears by the score, clowns and many other articles too numerous to mention. It was a veritable Father Christmas' grotto and quite unique – one could almost imagine St Niklas sitting in a corner of the room waiting for the children to whom he could distribute gifts to delight from that abundance of treasures.

My bedroom was also the repository for all of Ad's wide range of research records concerning World War II in the Netherlands. It is a mine of information and historical facts, mainly into the demise of many British servicemen. He has also researched and written several articles of events relating to the liberation period in the Autumn of 1944 and at that time was working on the liberation of his home town of Rosmalen, which was taken by the 53rd Welsh Division.

Another of his activities is the annual Eindhoven liberation celebrations which every September see the return of hundreds of veterans from Britain who helped to bring freedom to the first large town in the Netherlands to see the back of the Hun. His interests bring him correspondence from Australia, New Zealand, Canada and the United Kingdom. His latest project was the investigation of the crash of a Lancaster bomber in the town of Gemert, when all the crew perished. The story is worth the telling for it indicates the dedication of this man in his efforts to return something to the families of those who gave their lives for his country.

On July 20th 1944 a Lancaster Bomber was returning from a mission over Germany. When approaching the town of Gemert it was attacked by a Junker 88G night fighter. The Lancaster was hit and it exploded and the debris from it brought about the destruction of its attacker, the JU88. The debris of the Lancaster was spread over a large area, as were what remained of the bodies of the crew. Visiting the scene of the crash the next day, a young Dutch girl called Stien saw hanging from the branch of a nearby tree a silver bracelet, upon which was engraved the name 'Harvey'. Thinking that this might be something to do with the crashed plane she took it home. Her father, in turn, went to the Capucijnen Fathers in Handel where he handed over the silver bracelet. The Fathers contacted the local Red Cross who, as soon as it was practicable, approached the Royal Air Force. Their subsequent investigations revealed that the bracelet belonged to the pilot of the Lancaster, Pilot Officer Jack Harvey, who was a Canadian. Shortly after the war the bracelet was returned to his family in Canada and there it remained until 1993.

With the assistance of Ad Hermens, Jack Harvey's sister – Fay Wigelsworth, of Alberta – visited the Netherlands and met for the first time the now mature and married Dutch lady, Mvrow Stien Slits, who had found the bracelet almost fifty years ago. In the privacy of that Dutch lady's home, Fay Wigelsworth returned her brother's bracelet to Stien for permanent safe-keeping in the Netherlands.

Jack Harvey's mother, at that time past the age of ninety years, sent a message to the Dutch friends at a gathering in the Town Hall of Gemert when Mrs Wigelsworth was received and entertained by the Burgemeester. In appreciation for all his work connected with his research into this heartwarming story, Fay presented Ad Hermens with her brother Jack's original medals to add to his collection of memorabilia relating to the crashed Lancaster.

Of the remaining six crew members, two were Canadian and the rest British. After many hours of research Ad Hermans was able to trace the family of Johnny Loveridge, the rear gunner, to Portland, Hampshire, and was happy to arrange for the family to visit Gemert in September 1994, where they experienced the kind of welcome and hospitality that had been afforded to Fay Wigelsworth.

During my brief stay the weather in Geldrop was so warm that we were able to take all our meals, including breakfast, under the sun umbrella in the garden. There was always much good humour in that household – both Ad and Pia were very congenial companions, always ready with a joke, for laughter came easily to them.

The day I arrived was the birthday of Queen Beatrix. Many houses had the national flag flying as a sign of loyalty, something never seen in England. Ad explained to me that those houses who had done the job properly had also an orange flag flying alongside the national ensign to indicate allegiance to the House of Orange.

On Friday afternoon Ad and I went into the centre of Geldrop to watch the birthday celebrations, the main event of which was a bicycle race around a circuit in the town centre. I thought how appropriate that was for the country where the bicycle predominates over all other forms of conveyance. The locals certainly appeared to be enjoying themselves, with everyone well behaved. From there we journeyed to Mierlo Cemetery where two members of the 44th RTR are buried – Corporal Ralph Stothard and Trooper Basil Nicholls, both killed at Nuenen on September 20th 1944. There is a special memorial to them in the town of Nuenen at the spot where they met their deaths; a kindly gesture by whoever built it. Ad is also closely connected with Mierlo Cemetery and the annual service which takes place there every September. Our afternoon trip ended with a visit to a working windmill, a rare sight in the Netherlands these days. It was situated in a very beautiful setting, its finely balanced sails turning lazily despite the fact that there was hardly any breeze.

Alas came Saturday morning when I had to take my leave of Papenvoort and dear Moppie, who wanted her Engelsman to stay. Ad and Pia took me by car to St Oedenrode, just a few kilometres distant, where I was to stay with the van Weert family who had generously offered to accommodate me. We arrived at the home of Dorus, the man who had buried John, and his wife Mien. This was a pleasant cottage on de Ollandseweg, where we were greeted most warmly by those delightful people. Soon we were joined by Toon, Anneke and Henri their son; and not long afterwards by Louis Kleijne, the Head of Kienehoefschool, with whom it was my first meeting.

In no time at all coffee and cakes were on the table and once more in that pleasant company I participated in the 11am ritual. It was an enjoyable repast with nine people, one a welcome foreigner, all busily chattering away ten to the dozen and laughing when mouths were not full of delicious Dutch pastries.

It had been arranged that I would sleep at the home of Dorus and Mien, but I was to share my time and meals with both van Weert families whose homes were only two hundred metres apart. This turned out to be an excellent arrangement; both families were most hospitable and I thoroughly enjoyed my time with them. At breakfast, when I was without an interpreter in the form of Henri, I made every effort to understand Mien who in an attempt to make me feel at home, with smiles and gestures, spoke rapidly in Dutch. This left me scrambling in my brain for the odd word I remembered from my long hours of study. But we managed to communicate somehow and I lacked nothing in the way of food and comforts.

One amusing incident was when my special diet rye bread, a supply of which I had brought with me to last for several days, did not appear on the table. Mien had thought it too stale for me to eat so she gave it to the rabbits. I must admit that it was past its best and Mien had my best interests at heart; I only hope the rabbits survived. In the living room of that cosy Dutch home there is a framed photograph of John beside which Mien regularly places a vase of flowers. What a thoughtful and kindly act.

On Sunday Henri, accompanied by Toon and Anneke, took me on a tour of the surrounding countryside and on to Veghel to see Henri's place of work. This was followed by a visit to the excellent museum which portrays in great detail the 'Market Garden' operation including a street scene in which British armour and US paratroopers are displayed liberating a Dutch village, with the local populace welcoming their arrival. We spent almost two hours there, which was followed by an afternoon coffee in the restaurant.

On returning to St Oedenrode we were diverted to make an unexpected call, for me at least, to the home of Oda and Jan, Toon and Anneke's daughter and son-in-law. There a delicious meal had been prepared for us, mainly cooked by Jan who I believe likes to get his hand into the culinary side of kitchen activity.

On Monday I went to the home of Ad (Ben van Uden's youngest son) and his wife Toos, in the Griegstraat and met their four lovely children. In the afternoon Henri, Toon and I went on another tour of Noord Brabant, passing on the way the site of the windmill which had been used as a German observation post in September 1944 and which had been destroyed by John's seventeen pounder gun. From there we went to a clog factory, one of the few left in the Netherlands, but which is now merely a museum.

On our return we called at the Brabant Museum in Kirkstraat. The costumes on display reminded me very much of my first days in St Oedenrode when such apparel was still widely worn, especially by the old ladies of the town. Afterwards I bought some flowers which I placed on the grave of Louis and Jeanny Kleijne's son Maurice, who tragically lost his life in August 1992 in a road traffic accident. It was Maurice who often attended to the graves of the twenty three soldiers buried in the churchyard.

I have always found the food in Dutch homes both appetizing and filling, and it is never rationed. With the van Weerts I was introduced to a quite unusual, at least for me, Brabant speciality. This was made of mashed potatoes and meat, served with salad and liberal slices of various cooked meats, plus a dressing of pickles of various kinds. It tasted very good indeed and had it not been for the fact that I was so full of cakes and coffee I might have done the meal greater justice. Nevertheless, it was a new gastronomical pleasure which I have now enjoyed on two occasions; once with Mien and once at Anneke's home.

Tuesday May 4th was a very busy day with tight schedules to be observed. Louis Kleijne came to pick me up from Dorus and Mien's home at about 10.30am, just in time for morning coffee. We then went to the Kienehoefschool where, in honour of my visit, the Union Jack was flying alongside the Dutch flag. The thought did occur to me that this was possibly the only time in my life when such a courtesy would be paid to me, so it was indeed a moment to savour.

I was ushered into the hall where fifty one children were sitting in a large circle awaiting my arrival. What immediately impressed me was their impeccable behaviour – no rowdiness or indiscipline was apparent, they just looked to be a very happy group of children. They were in the age range of ten to thirteen years and were studying English.

Louis made a brief speech by way of introduction, after which I spoke to them in Dutch from a prepared speech. Credit for that, however badly delivered it might have been, must go to Henri who had some weeks previously kindly translated my English version into good Dutch, which it would have been beyond my knowledge of the language to have done. He did assure me later, from the video made of my visit, that it sounded not too bad; at least they all understood it. Whether the children were impressed I will never know, but they did clap politely and

I think with a little enthusiasm.

The whole point of my visit, as mentioned earlier, was to make the children understand the importance of peace in the world. Also for them to be aware of the sadness war brings to all sides in a conflict, of the freedom they now enjoy in consequence of the liberation of their country in 1944-45. I had no part in that event and I had suggested to Louis before I came to the school that one of his 'Market Garden' veterans would be far better qualified to talk about it. They also wanted to know the part my family had played in the war and to answer prepared questions about brother John. This was to be part of their project to honour his memory.

Under the direction of their Headmaster and his Deputy, H Vonk, each child in turn then asked me their prepared question. These included: what John and I did before the war, how we got on as brothers, our work, hobbies, what I felt when he was killed, what effect it had on my family and how did I feel now about the Germans who had been responsible for his death. Very searching enquiries, but I think I managed to cope with them satisfactorily.

At the end of the questioning Louis thanked me for coming to the school and then said that the children had something for me. To my utter amazement, surprise and bewilderment, the children then lined up and each one presented me with a red rose. Attached to each flower was a card, designed by the individual child, on which was written a message in honour of John; each was signed by the donor.

As each child approached me to present their rose I tried to thank them but words did not come easily. My smile, I hope, made up for my loss of words. To think that these youngsters should be so caring about the events of so long ago made me feel very humble. I will long remember that day – it was unique and very special for me. If only my mother could have shared it with me.

The flowers were later that day shared between the graves of John and Stanley Matthews in Uden Cemetery. The labels were, at my request, removed later by Ties Verstegen and kept for me so that I have a record of the names of all those Dutch children:

Carla Arts	Ruud Maas
Elske van Asseldonk	Natasje Mimpen
Wim Biemans	Marjon Minneboo
Johnny van de Biggelaar	Marleen Plaat
Martine van de Burgt	Sandra van de Putten
Audry Coppens	Heidi Raaymakers
Ellen van Dam	Tom Raaymakers
Michiel Dam	Brigitte Rampelt
Birgit Daniels	Emmy Rooyackers
Linda van Dijk	Maartje Saris
Sjoerd Eijkemans	Anke Smits
Sjors van Erp	Lennie Smits
Anke Habraken	Maico Verhagen
Niels van de Heijden	Carin Vermeltfoort
Noortje van de Heuvel	Marieke Vermeltfoort
Nancy van de Heyden	Debbie Vervoort
John Heymans	Sanne Vervoort
Esther Hol	Eric Vervoort
Marnon Huibers	Melanie van Vugt
Joost van Kampen	Kim Vulders
Joost Kapteijns	Emiel van de Wetering
Joyce Koolen	Paul van de Wetering
Wieteke Kuipers	Jan van de Wiel
Evelien Lafleur	Jeroen van Wijk
Anne Latijnhouwers	Maartje de Wit
Laura Loerakker	

After lunch with Louis and Jeanny we went to the cemetery in the grounds of the local Roman Catholic church in the centre of the town. There are twenty three graves of British soldiers buried in that graveyard. They lie in a circle around a shrub covered mound which is surmounted by the statue of a saint – St Martin, I presume, after whom the church is named. All these men were killed during the liberation of St Oedenrode and their bodies were not moved to the main collecting cemetery at Uden, where the majority of men who died in this area of Noord Brabant have their final resting place. Before I arrived in the Netherlands I had written to Louis and had suggested it might be fitting if during the service of remembrance which was to take place one of the children of the 'liberated' wore John's medals. The demand from the children was so enthusiastic that Louis decided that a ballot, for one boy and one girl to wear them, would be the fairest way to decide.

At the cemetery we were joined by Ad and Pia, who had travelled from Geldrop to share with us this unique service, Ad also bringing his video recorder to make a film of the event. Anneke, Toon, Henri and Dorus also arrived to join the congregation. The colourfully dressed children of the Kienehoefschool came in two parties, each child carrying a bunch of flowers to place on a particular grave. The children then stood in a group before the graves and were given by their Headmaster a brief history of almost every soldier. He went from grave to grave as he related how each one had met his death; knowledge he had gained from research over several years. He reminded the children as they stood there in the warm spring sunshine, with the right to say, to think and to do what they liked, that this was due to the sacrifice made by those men who had liberated their country. He added that although there were only twenty three men in that cemetery there were many thousands upon thousands buried elsewhere in the

Netherlands, who had given their lives for the freedom of other people.

The children then moved to their allotted places around the circle of graves and together walked forward and placed their flowers at the foot of each headstone. This was followed by a minute's silence interrupted only by the singing of the birds in the trees. In the first group of children Carla Arts wore John's medals and separately laid flowers to his memory on one of the nearby graves. This ceremony was repeated by the second group of children and the posy for John was laid by the bemedalled Joost Kapteijns. It was a very moving occasion for all of us and everyone was most impressed with the attitude of the children, all of whom behaved very graciously and in a manner befitting such a ceremony. I am sure they will remember it long into their adult life.

As a token of my appreciation I sent to Louis Kleijne a copy of that excellent book entitled *Courage Remembered*, published by HM Stationary Office. This is an account of the War Graves Commission throughout the world written jointly by T A Edwin Gibson and G Kingsley Wood. Louis had asked me to record on its flyleaf an account of my visit. This is what I wrote:

> This book is presented to Louis Kleijne, Headmaster of the Kienehoefschool, St Oedenrode, in appreciation and grateful thanks to him, his staff and the pupils of the school, for keeping alive the memory of those soldiers of the allied forces who died during the liberation of St Oedenrode in September 1944.
>
> In particular for their remarkable and unique tribute on 4th May 1993, to my brother, 7946671, Trooper John Frederick Thorogood (Gunner) of 'C' Squadron, 44th Royal Tank Regiment, 4th Armoured Brigade, who at the age of twenty one, after years of active service in North Africa, Sicily and Italy, the invasion of Normandy in June 1944 and the liberation of France and Belgium, was killed in action during

the afternoon of 21st September 1944, on de Ollandseweg, near the home of the family van Weert, together with his comrade, 79103 Trooper Stanley Matthews (Driver), aged twenty two. They died attempting to repulse a German attack on 'The Corridor' during operation 'Market Garden'. From 21st September 1944 until 12th June 1946, both soldiers were buried on the roadside until their interment in Uden Commonwealth War Cemetery, where they lie side by side in Plot 1, Row D, graves 4 and 5.

I shall ever be grateful to you all and treasure the memory of my unforgettable visit to Kienehoefschool and the smiling faces of the children who I hope will long remember and cherish the experience we shared on that memorable day.

And now it was time for me to say goodbye to Ad and Pia, who headed back to Geldrop for they were unable to leave Moppie alone for too long (sadly, she died the following September a few days after her ninetieth birthday). They had been marvellous hosts and nothing had been too much trouble for them. I then returned to the Kleijne home, along with Major Bob Lockwood, Royal Signals, who had travelled from his unit in Germany for this service. From there Henri collected me to convey me to Uden, my next port of call. I had of course said my goodbyes, and expressed my thanks, to Dorus and Mien earlier in the day. They had been excellent hosts and had shown me much kindness during my brief but enjoyable stay with them.

And so, accompanied by Toon and Anneke, it was goodbye once more to St Oedenrode, a place of great significance to me, and on to Uden, another town of equal importance. There I was delivered safe and sound to Jan and Stine at whose home in St Annastraat I was to stay for the remainder of my time in the Netherlands.

That evening we all attended the annual commemoration service in Uden church close by the Commonwealth War

Cemetery. Unfortunately I was separated from my Dutch friends as being a British guest of the Uden War Cemetery Foundation I had to join the other visitors in the front pews which had been reserved for us. The service was attended by the Burgemeester of Uden and his wife, along with many local dignitaries. All those energetic and devoted people whose efforts make this annual service possible were also present, with Ties Verstegen watching over the proceedings.

I joined up with Bob Lockwood, who had also travelled from St Oedenrode to attend this service – his uncle is buried in the cemetery just a few rows behind John's grave. The service was beyond anything either of us had expected. The church was packed to capacity with Dutch people and in addition to the two orchestras there was a mixed choir which sang several beautiful English ballads – in English, I should add. They and the orchestras performed admirably. The service was conducted in both English and Dutch. It was indeed a remarkable experience and one felt humility for this exceptional tribute to our men. The service, which stirred emotions in us all, ended with the singing of our national anthems.

That was not the end of it; the service was followed by a wreath laying ceremony in the cemetery across the road. The congregation, led by the British visitors, was preceded by a local band playing a slow march, to which we walked at pace. Not only had the church been packed to capacity but outside many more townsfolk had gathered to take part in the final stage of the commemoration service. On entering the cemetery I noticed that Jan had once more placed posies of flowers on the graves of John and Stan, to which had been added the fifty one red roses presented by the children of the Kienehoefschool.

The many hundreds in the congregation gathered in the cemetery facing the Cross of Sacrifice which was bounded by the flags of Britain and the Netherlands, fluttering proudly in the breeze. Many beautiful wreaths were laid from several branches of local society; the Town Council, the Royal Netherlands Air Force representing the military and the Royal British Legion. The last post was sounded, followed by the silence and reveille. It was a fitting end to what had been for everyone present a most moving and memorable occasion.

I said my farewells to Toon, Anneke, Henri and Louis Kleijne, who had motored from St Oedenrode after close of school to join in the service. I was sorry to see them all depart for they had treated me so well during my stay in their town – they had all been perfect hosts and everything for my benefit had been arranged without a hitch of any kind. Henri, for much of my time in St Oedenrode, was a constant companion, doing most of the translating when necessary and driving me wherever I needed to go.

Happily, in September 1992, we had been delighted to play host for a day to the van Weert clan when they took a day off from their holiday in North Wales to visit us in Solihull. It was a very busy and, we particularly hope for them, enjoyable few hours. A trip to Henley-in-Arden and Warwick Castle was fitted in after lunch.

At Uden the British visitors enjoyed with their Dutch hosts a very pleasant evening at a local restaurant, 'd'n Vorstenburg', when speeches were made by both sides. This concluded, for the British especially, a most memorable visit to the land of flowers. The Burgemeester, K Hehenkamp, referred in his closing address to the flags of both nations which had flanked the Cross of Sacrifice that day, and he expressed the hope that they would always fly side by side in friendship. We all silently agreed with that sentiment.

And so back to St Annastraat, where my usual room awaited me. Again it was a case of home from home for Jan and Stine, my very good friends for over thirty years, have always welcomed me most warmly whenever I arrived on their doorstep. They never seem to age and Jan amazed me with his vigour and good humour. On Wednesday morning Jan took me to the Volkel Airfield, a base of the Royal Netherlands Air Force. The reason for our visit was to examine the war diary of a particular Royal Air Force squadron which had operated from Volkel in February 1945 during the closing stages of the war. We were attempting to prove the truth, or otherwise, of a supposedly authentic story related in a book as to certain events which were alleged to have taken place on that airfield on February 9th and 10th 1945.

The story told how a certain Squadron Leader had been killed in attempting to land his damaged Tempest on returning from a sortie. Also, that he had been buried on the day following the crash, February 10th, in a temporary grave in Volkel churchyard. Had such an interment taken place the body of that officer would have been reinterred in Uden cemetery, but it wasn't; hence our enquiry. Jan had arranged with the RNAF for us to meet a Dutch officer from the base who would conduct us to the museum on the airfield which was to be opened especially for us – it is usually open to the public only on certain days of the year.

Lodged in the museum were duplicate war diaries of all the Royal Air Force squadrons which had operated from Volkel at that time in 1945 and these were made available for our examination. The diary of the squadron revealed that no such officer had been killed on that day, that no sorties whatever were flown on February 9th, due to bad weather, and that no such officer ever served with the squadron. Another intriguing story.

Needless to say, we were given every cooperation by our helpful conducting officer who drew our attention to many interesting aspects of the memorabilia on display. The museum was divided into three sections. The first related to the German Air Force, who built it, and its pilots whose photographs and log books were on display. Similar information was shown about the British Royal Air Force who had three squadrons operating from Volkel during the last months of the war. The officer mentioned that they had been given a great deal of help from former RAF flyers to obtain records and equipment to furnish the museum with such an impressive display. It was fascinating to see the amount of material which formed an excellent historical record of the dramatic days of 1945, when operations from that airfield helped to bring about the defeat of the Thousand Year Reich.

In the afternoon I visited Ties Verstegen and his wife and spent a very enjoyable hour or two with them. This included an inspection of his very extensive system of records about the cemetery, in which he shows such great interest. He had many files of correspondence with relatives from all over the Commonwealth, the next of kin of the fallen, many albums of photographs of the cemetery going back to the time it was first opened, and extensive information about the men buried there. He devotes much of his free time to this work and derives much satisfaction from his role as self appointed curator.

Ties accompanied me back to St Annastraat and we called on the way at the home of a Dutch lady who was hosting English visitors from Castle Bromwich. No sooner had I sat down to chat with these people, who seemed to be having an enjoyable time, than I had placed before me a cup of coffee and a huge slice of apple tart. Reluctantly, and feeling somewhat embarrassed, I had to refuse for but a few minutes previously I had been obliged to take cake and coffee at Ties Verstegen's, and that after a substantial lunch at St Annastraat. This coffee and cakes business was getting quite beyond my capacity to cope with, despite the fact that I do not have a slimming problem. But so much for Dutch hospitality.

On Thursday Jan, now past his eightieth year but looking a sprightly sixty, decided that we should go on a grand day tour of the more northern part of his country in the direction of Apeldoorn. It was a beautiful day, like all the days during my visit, and we passed through many towns and villages of antiquity and interest. The most fabulous was Het Loo, built by William of Orange the Stedholder, which was magnificent and has a most beautiful garden. Through his marriage to Mary, the eldest daughter of James II of England, he became William III of England, holding the throne jointly with his wife. James II had been an unpopular monarch because of his attempt to reintroduce the Roman Catholic faith in England against the general wishes of the people. He was deposed in 1688 in what was to become known as 'The Glorious Revolution' because of the lack of bloodshed. William landed at Brixham in Devon, where his statue overlooks the harbour. He marched unopposed to London where he and Mary reigned and ensured that Protestantism continued; they were popular rulers.

After a coffee break in the lavishly furnished and chandeliered restaurant, another unrivalled experience, we motored on to Harderwijk via Udiel, Elspet, Nunspeet and Elberg, crossing over the bridge to Oosterlijk Flevoland (the land below the sea). At Harderwijk Jan and Stine kindly took me to a restaurant for lunch where they introduced me to a Dutch speciality of fried eels with salad, french fries and vegetables; a very unusual but tasty dish which I ate with relish. I have, however, yet to find the courage to eat a raw salted herring.

On Thursday May 7th, my last day in the Netherlands, Jan had insisted despite my protestations that he take me to Eindhoven airport. I would have been quite happy to have taken the bus from Uden but he would brook no argument about it, so it was agreed that he would personally 'see me off the premises'.

During the morning of departure Jan and I went to a local farm where we purchased a large supply of excellent asparagus, some of which I brought home with me together with some free range eggs from the hens which could be seen scratching round the farmyard. Returning to Uden I made a last visit to the cemetery for a quiet moment of contemplation, reassuring myself that I would return another year. After that a quick trip to the local shopping centre for a supply of the delicious smoked ham which is so popular with my family but unobtainable at home. Our lunch at St Annastraat included a generous portion of delicious asparagus swimming in butter; it is invariably on the menu.

Later in the afternoon we set off from Uden, following the old 'Corridor' (it later also became known as 'Hell's Highway') to Eindhoven airport. What a beautiful part of the country it is, with everywhere looking so spruce and prosperous. There are no signs anywhere to remind one of the killings which took place along that road in 1944 and which, in the event, brought early liberation to that part of Noord Brabant.

At the airport I bade farewell to my good friends Jan and Stine who, yet again, repeated their invitation to return to their home in Uden at anytime where a bed would always be waiting for me – what more could anyone offer? I caught my plane at 5.40pm and after a brief flight arrived safely back at Birmingham airport to find my friend Larry waiting to convey me home.

It had been yet another visit full of unforgettable memories of people who spared no effort to dispense the kind of hospitality which had begun forty eight years earlier when I was a stranger in their midst. It is heartwarming to know that in spite of the passing of the years and the declining number of British visitors to the graves of their loved ones, the Dutch people continue to give freely not only the comfort of their homes but of their hearts as well.

The Final Tribute

THE PORT OF CALAIS WAS RECEDING INTO THE DISTANCE AS OUR CONVOY of four coaches from the Birmingham War Research Society headed towards the Netherlands. Dark clouds and driving rain presented a gloomy outlook. The majority of passengers, tired after a sleepless overnight journey from King's Norton, catnapped in their seats and a general quiet pervaded our coach. In this atmosphere of solitude, punctuated only by the noise as the wheels ploughed through the road surface water, I pondered on the events which found me heading for a rendezvous which some weeks earlier I could not possibly have foreseen.

It had been my intention since my last visit to go to the Netherlands for the fiftieth anniversary of 'Market Garden'. Both my elder son John and son-in-law Moayad had expressed a wish to accompany me. I had planned not to join them for the outward leg of the journey as I proposed to fly from Birmingham to Amsterdam and then make my way by public transport to St Oedenrode. Once there, in company with my local Dutch friends, I would lay a wreath on the spot in de

Ollandseweg where John had been found and meet up later with the coach party at the appointed hotel. I informed my Dutch friends and also Ian Alexander, co-proprietor of the society, and it was he who immediately offered to make a detour to take in a visit to St Oedenrode as part of the itinerary for that trip. He observed that he could drop off the other passengers in the marketplace where they could have coffee while we proceeded to de Ollandseweg to lay the British Legion poppy wreath. The saving of an air fare was certainly a consideration so I accepted his generous proposal and advised my Dutch friends of this revised arrangement.

Almost simultaneously there arrived from Louis Kleijne, that energetic and dedicated Headmaster (and craftsman to boot), a letter reminding me that some five years previously I had briefly mentioned to Ad Hermens the possibility of placing a plaque along de Ollandseweg to the memory of John and Stanley. Knowing the problems of obtaining planning permission for such a memorial the matter had never been pursued as a serious possibility. Now Louis was writing to say he intended to design and produce such a small memorial and he hoped it would be ready in time for my visit. My surprise can well be imagined, especially following upon a letter I had received a few days previously from a Mr L Mee – Chairman of the Royal British Legion, Austin Branch in Northfield, Birmingham – informing me that he and other members had been so moved by the article about John by Graham Young which had appeared in the D Day Supplement of the Birmingham Evening Mail, that during a recent visit to the Arnhem and Nijmegen areas they had diverted their coach to Uden. There at the military cemetery they had held a special service at John's grave with all the panoply associated with Legion gatherings. A selection of excellent photographs of the event accompanied his letter.

My excitement at this latest prospect was heightened by Ian's later suggestion to take all four coaches to witness the event. My mind boggled at the thought of four large coaches with over two hundred people aboard descending upon a small gathering in that rural part of the town. My Dutch friends, I imagine, were equally taken aback for Louis telephoned me urgently requesting me to confirm that four coaches were in fact to arrive, since he needed to advise the local police of the coming invasion.

So here I was, quietly reflecting upon our arrival at St Oedenrode, scheduled for 10.30am, the centre of attention of four coach loads of British veterans. These included airborne and representatives of many other arms of the services who took part in 'Market Garden', their families and others interested in the epic events of those momentous days of September 1944. Would we arrive on time? I imagined people waiting in the rain and getting drenched for there appeared to be no let up in the miserable conditions. It had been mentioned that a brief ceremony would be held although exactly what form this would take was a matter of conjecture. But knowing my Dutch friends I felt no unease or discomfort; I had known them long enough to appreciate and value the warmth which would greet my arrival. We passed the outskirts of Eindhoven and linked up with the road leading to Son, St Oedenrode and beyond which in September 1944 had become known as 'The Corridor' or 'Hell's Highway'. Upon that single narrow winding country road it had been the height of folly for the British High Command to attempt to push forward a whole Corps of British troops with the aim of reaching Arnhem in forty eight hours. Any breakdown could result in a major delay and unfortunately experience proved this to be the case. In addition, attacks by German Divisions from the flanks further delayed the progress of the relieving forces.

Now, as we approached St Oedenrode, crossing over the Son

bridge (scene of heavy fighting on September 17th when the bridge was blown by the Germans which delayed the initial advance) I went to the front of the coach to direct the convoy through St Oedenrode itself. The main road, now so neat and tidy, contrasted sharply with what I remembered from my visit in November 1945 when the debris of war and numerous wayside graves were evidence of the fierce fighting which had taken place in that area. Approaching the town we turned left into Nijnselweg, negotiating our way carefully through the narrow streets leading to the market place. St Oedenrode is a bustling, prosperous town and our progress through it was somewhat delayed by the traffic congestion, one delivery van holding us up for some minutes. At times it was indeed a narrow squeeze between parked cars as the convoy attempted to make headway without damaging local property. At 10.40am, just ten minutes late, we turned into de Ollandseweg, the final lap of the long journey from Calais; not bad timing considering the weather and traffic delays. The rain was still beating down and the window wipers on our lead coach were functioning at top speed. Soon, in the distance, between the rows of trees bounding the road, we observed a splash of colour highlighting the dark overcast surroundings. As we got nearer, loud cheering voices could be heard and miniature Dutch flags were being waved vigorously by the hands of many children. And there on the right hand side of the road, half concealed by the congregation, was a large Dutch flag standing tall above the multitude, damp but proud.

 The first person I recognised was the bearded Louis, decidedly wet, bare headed and clad in a blue anorak. He was happily waving a greeting and directing us to turn left into Rijsingen, the long drive leading to the van Weert home, which quite comfortably accommodated two of the buses. The Master of Ceremonies in parking was Toon van Weert who, wearing traditional Dutch clogs, efficiently directed the vehicles between the neighbouring buildings and trim hedges.

Being the first to alight I was soon besieged by my many friends who under the shelter of their umbrellas greeted me enthusiastically, firm handshakes from the men, hugs and kisses from all the delightful ladies. But it was all so hurried and confusing and I had little time to talk with everyone. An introduction to Meneer P Schriek, the Burgemeester, was both an unexpected and a pleasant surprise – to be so honoured by his presence made me feel like visiting royalty. Also present were two former GI's of the 101st US Airborne Division. They were Captain Fred Hancock from Long Beach California, now aged eighty four, who had commanded 'C' Company of the 502nd Regiment which liberated the centre of St Oedenrode; and ex Sergeant Cam Anderson of Columbia Tennessee, also of 'C' Company. Both were guests of Louis and Jeanny at their nearby home in Cathalijnepad. It was a pleasure to meet them and I wished I could have chatted to them for a while, but time was short. Over the years many ex GI's of the 'Screaming Eagles' have visited St Oedenrode which they rightly acknowledge as a place of special pilgrimage – they had lost many comrades in liberating the town, which always receives them with great warmth.

Then I saw Ad Hermens, without whose efforts none of this would have happened. He was the instigator of this exceptional relationship which has built up in recent years. He presented me with his recently published book *Rosmalen in de Vuurlinie*, a story covering the battle for the liberation of his birthplace of Rosmalen. In addition to all my friends many local people had gathered who, with the added numbers of our party of British visitors, swelled the crowd to several hundred. Such a gathering had perhaps never before been seen along de Ollandseweg.

After renewing friendships, albeit briefly, with my many close

Dutch friends, Louis invited me, my son John and Dorus van Weert to stand before the memorial plinth which was situated just inside the front garden of the home of the Schepens family and near to the spot where Dorus had found John. The memorial was covered with the union flag. Louis made a very moving speech of welcome in which he referred to the sacrifices made by the liberating allied forces, but said that on that day they especially wished to remember and honour John Thorogood and Stanley Matthews. He added that the memorial would be a permanent reminder to everyone in the area that the cost of freedom fifty years earlier had been the lives of such young men and he expressed the hope that the peace which such sacrifice had brought would continue for many years to come.

Louis then requested me to remove the flag and hand it to him. The first sight of the memorial moved me deeply – an upright pillar about one metre tall fashioned from Indonesian hardwood, with a floral carving of roses on its front forming the design, the flowers supporting the base of a bronze plaque upon which the names of the two soldiers encircled the badge of the Royal Tank Regiment, below which were the words 'HUN JONGE LEVEN HIER GEVEN' (They gave their young lives here). It was a beautiful piece of craftsmanship, fashioned personally by Louis in his home workshop. I was indeed surprised for I had not expected anything quite like it. Everything about it reflected the dedication and depth of feeling which had brought about its creation, but especially the roses, symbol of love and new life, lifting upward and supporting the names of the dead. Dorus then stepped forward and placed the British Legion Cross of Poppies at the foot of the plinth. Attached to it was a photograph of both soldiers taken in front of their tank surrounded by several enthusiastic liberated citizens of the town of St Niklas in Belgium some days before they met their end. This was followed by the laying of floral tributes from Ad and Pia, Anneke, Toon and Henri, Dorus and Mien, Louis and Jeanny, Buurtvereniging 'Oud Rijsigen' and many others to whom I shall always be indebted. I was approached by Mr and Mrs Schepens who said they were honoured to have the plinth sited in their garden, where it would be tended with devotion and care in the years ahead. It was an emotional moment, but the smiles and hand claps quickly brought me back to reality for I too had words of thanks to express and so there was no time for indulging in depressing thoughts. This was an occasion which had brought us together in friendship to share a very special experience – the honouring of two quite ordinary soldiers.

I hope they understood my brief speech of thanks in Dutch, rendered with a pronounced English accent as Henri would no doubt rightly tell me. But if composition, delivery and accent was in need of improvement the words were well meant. This was followed by some words in English for the benefit of my fellow travellers who had witnessed a very moving and unusual scene. There were veterans present who were already aware from their own wartime experiences in the Netherlands of the kindness and hospitality of the Dutch people, but for any first time visitors it must have been a revelation. Memorials and the like are usually reserved for those of exalted rank and station in life. There they had witnessed such a compliment being paid to two unknown young troopers, albeit long serving veterans of other campaigns abroad, who had met their untimely end at the ages of twenty one and twenty two in this quiet corner of the Netherlands and whose memories were now being perpetuated for many years into the future by their liberated hosts.

Sadly the time came to depart, for our tour operators had to visit other venues. Quick handshakes, smiles, muttered words of farewell, all quite inadequate for the occasion, had to suffice, but a promise was made to renew our friendship in May 1995 when the Netherlands would joyfully celebrate the fiftieth anniversary of their liberation.

So, waving to my many friends who now stood quietly in the driving rain, our convoy slowly accelerated forward leaving behind the warm-hearted Dutch congregation with whom we had just shared a very special and unique moment in time. We also left behind us a reminder of the result of 'Market Garden', where miscalculation, poor intelligence and hurried decisions had culminated in the defeat and death of many of the gallant beleaguered British and Polish airborne troops at Arnhem, and thousands more of equally brave American and British soldiers like John and Stan who died attempting to reach them.

But on the credit side was the liberation of the South Netherlands, through which we were now travelling on our way to Uden. Just beyond St Oedenrode was the hamlet of Koevering where forty nine years earlier on the land of farmer William van Tanden I came across the two tanks of 'C' Squadron commanded by Sergeants Worley and Newman. They were destroyed on September 25th 1944 at a cost of six lives. It was on a similar day in November, but much colder, that Ben van Uden and I had trudged for hours over fields in search of John's tank, but had found only these two. Further, it was near Koevering that the German thrust from the flanks breached 'The Corridor' on September 24th and delayed the relieving forces for forty eight hours. By that time it was all but over for the airborne troops at Arnhem.

Soon we entered Uden and there waiting to greet us, as always, were our dear friends Jan and Stine Heesen, Ties Verstegen, son Jack, and Paul Verbakel of the Foundation. Prior to our arrival they had placed flowers upon John and Stan's graves to which I added the poppy wreath which throughout the remembrance year 1992/93 had lain at the foot of the 44th

RTR memorial tablet at the TAVR Centre in Bristol. This I had recovered after the final reunion with the intention of placing it in Uden cemetery. To mark the occasion of the 'Market Garden' anniversary, the Union and Dutch flags were flying at the entrance while in the central reservation at the first grave of each row had been placed vases of freshly cut flowers which gave a blaze of colour against the damp sombre autumn morning. I presumed this was the work of the Foundation, with Ties to the fore with the arrangements. They are already planning for May 1995 and are hoping for good support from the many British friends whose numbers are unfortunately slowly on the decline with the passing of the years.

The remainder of our brief stay was taken up with tours in the Arnhem and Oosterbeek areas, including a visit to the Hartenstein Hotel Museum, Oosterbeek cemetery and Ginkel Heath, where we witnessed the commemoration drop by paratroopers of the armed services. It was at Ginkel Heath that we were entertained by the pipes and drums of the 48th Netherlands Highlanders, an unusual sight indeed as they marched off to commands in English to the rousing tune of *Scotland the Brave*. On to the Reichwald War Cemetery near Kleve in Germany, where a brief remembrance service was held preceded by a parade of veterans; this included former members of the Parachute Regiment from Scotland who were in out party. The drill was a little rusty but spirits were high. When returning to our hotel in Sevenum we called at the Groesbeek Cemetery which is the resting place for the many Canadians of all services who fell in the Netherlands and neighbouring parts of Germany. Here, as elsewhere throughout our trip, crowds of sympathetic Dutch of all ages were eager to talk to us and to express their appreciation for their liberation. The atmosphere everywhere was one of close friendship with people waving from the windows and doorways of their homes, many displaying the flags of both nations. People lined the streets, despite the awful weather, awaiting parades or the arrival of the convoy of around four hundred second world war vehicles, and they broke into smiles and gave signs of welcome when they recognised coaches from Britain. It was a foretaste of the kind of hospitality I imagine will herald the liberation celebrations an 1995; they will be euphoric and I would not miss sharing in their joy.

A visit to the Bevrijdingsmuseum in Groesbeek gave further evidence of the dedication of the Dutch nation to honour the war-dead. Within its cloisters in a circular room, under a canopy roof shaped like a parachute, are comprehensive records for every allied serviceman – whether American, British, Canadian, Dutch or Polish – who fell in the campaign to liberate North West Europe. Every Corps, Division, Brigade, Regiment or Service is listed. The registers also show, where known, the date and place of death and place of burial. Such a list in respect of the casualties suffered by 44th RTR is shown in the appendices at the back of this book. A truly prodigious achievement for the compilers of such a remarkable record, unequalled, I would imagine, anywhere else in the world.

Perhaps the most spontaneous and unexpected moment of our trip was during the closing hours of Sunday evening at our AC hotel, where the accommodation, food and service had been first class. We were coming to the end of our evening revelries when a young Dutch girl, attired in folk costume, entered the dining room. She asked if we would clear a space in the centre of the room as they wished to entertain us. We did not know quite what to expect; no doubt they had recognised us as British visitors. She was a member of 'De Dorsvlegels', a cabaret and folk dance group, and they had stopped off at the hotel for a coffee break while on their way home to Dongen after touring. Well, what a surprise we received when the entire group of twenty three – thirteen women and ten men – attired in full folk costume and comprising musicians, dancers and singers, began to entertain us. This was preceded by an announcement by their leader who said: 'Fifty years ago you came to help us gain our freedom. Now we will do something for you in return."

This, naturally, was received with great enthusiasm and we all applauded loudly. Soon they struck up their band with accordions, flutes, guitar and drums providing the music as the dancers and singers went into their numerous and enjoyable routines. Their songs were jolly even though we could not fully understand the words, but we got the general drift and clapped in time to the tunes to give them the support they so well deserved. This continued for about an hour or more, each turn being applauded more loudly than the last. A very good spirit charged the atmosphere, with British and Dutch enjoying this remarkable and impromptu gathering. Their excellent performance was followed by our Highland piper, Ian Alexander, taking up the pipes and playing many stirring wartime songs beginning with *Its a Long Way to Tipperary*, by which time we were all mixed up and conga-ing around the hotel dining room singing at the top of our voices. The songs seemed to be as familiar to the Dutch as they were to us for they sang *Tipperary* in English. Rousing Scottish marches followed, heightening the gaiety and enjoyment of the evening. One of the young Dutch girls, an accordionist, even played the bagpipes, which she did most competently with Ian providing the wind for the 'sack'. She got a well deserved cheer for that, and can been seen on video doing it.

The hotel manager, who so generously tolerated all this late hour revelry without a word of complaint, surpassed himself and became so enthusiastic that he offered free drinks all round. It was truly an evening to remember, and our stay could not have been more fittingly terminated. The joy and happiness we shared for a brief spell with that happy band of Dutch performers who, despite their fatigue and desire to get home to bed after a hectic tour, had stopped for a final curtain to give us pleasure will, I am sure, never be repeated. It will certainly be talked about in many a British home for a long time to come.

For all of us present it was the perfect ending to a remarkable and unforgettable long weekend when we had the pleasure of witnessing and sharing throughout the trip in the great spirit of friendship which exists between two peoples. Long may it be so for was it not the legendary General Hackett who, in a speech in Kate ter Horst's[1] house, spoke of 'Love springing from War'?

---

1 Known as 'The Angel of Arnhem'

Bibliography and Acknowledgements

Battlefields of Northern France and the Low Countries, by Michael Glover (pub. Michael Joseph)

Courage Remembered, by T A Edwin Gibson and G Kingsley Wood (pub. HMSO)

A History of the 44th Royal Tank Regiment 1939-45

The Devil's Birthday – The Bridges to Arnhem, by Geoffrey Powell (pub. Buchan & Enright)

Eindoll Maas, by Jack Diddon and Martin Swarts (pub. De Goosie Uitgeverij of Weep)

Brabant Bevrijd, by Jack Didden and Maarten Swarts (pub. van Geyt Productions)

Rendezvous With Destiny. A History of the American 101st Airborne Division, by Leonard Rapport and Arthur Northwood Jnr (pub. Association Airborne Division)

History of the 4th Dorsets, World War II

Prisoners of the Reich, by D Rolf (pub. Leo Cooper)

History of the 13th Hussars, with kind permission of Home HQ, The Light Division, York

Photographs of the Market-Place and Eerschot, St Oedenrode, and the Wim van Keulen story which appeared in the newspaper *Midden Brabant* are reproduced by kind permission of L P M Lieshout of St Oedenrode.

The map of Operation Market Garden is reproduced from *September 1944 Operation Market Garden* by A Korthals Altes, K Margry, G Thuring and R Voskuil (pub. Unieboek 1994)

Thanks are due he Bevrijdingsmuseum, Groesbeek, Nederland, for permission to publish the list of men of the 44th RTR killed in action in north west Europe, as compiled by J Hey

Appendix A

Some relevant extracts from the daily diary of sixty one year old Mary Ann Thorogood, beginning on January 8th 1942, the day John received his 'calling up' papers. The author found this diary among his mother's papers after her death on March 28th 1962.

JANUARY 8TH 1942
John received his 'calling up' papers. Didn't feel very cheerful for an hour or two but by the time John came home had got over it. In the evening went to the pictures.

JANUARY 15TH 1942
The day has arrived. I go with John to the station to see him off on his journey. Very cold indeed. Arrived home and felt very lonely. Went on duty from 2 until 10pm. Everyone very nice to me.

JANUARY 16TH 1942
A letter from the Paymaster to inform me I am not entitled to any allowances, only what John and George allow me.

JANUARY 20TH 1942
Took half an hour to get home through the snow, the snow over my knees. Received a letter from John and he is alright, so must post him a letter and cigs. Roads in terrible condition no papers, no milk or bread. Damned cold at post, no heat, no fuel.

JANUARY 21ST 1942
Weather still very cold, have been trying to get the old crystal set going, still persevering, wish I could get it to go to hear some news.

JANUARY 22ND 1942
Nothing extra special today, still very cold. No London Mail, milk a block of ice, a week today since John joined up. Longing for the time to go so as to have John home on leave, in about six weeks he says in his letter.

JANUARY 24TH 1942
Letter from John – sent cigs and stamps – registered as he did not receive the first parcel I sent.

JANUARY 29TH 1942
No letters yet but sent letter and cigs to John, also sent George a letter. Mail from India very bad.

FEBRUARY 9TH 1942
Registered letter from John with £1. Got home from duty 10.15pm. Niagara Falls – burst pipes in lavatory. Lovely mess, everywhere swimming.

FEBRUARY 10TH 1942
Sent cigs to John. Wrote to George. Today is my son's birthday (George's). God bless him he is 23 years old. Oh how thankful I shall be when I see him home again. Over two years since I saw him off to India. I do thank God for two good sons and pray God they will both come home again. God help and protect them wherever they are and keep them safe always.

FEBRUARY 23RD 1942
Received letter from John with £1 to treat myself. Wrote to John and sent cigs.

FEBRUARY 26TH 1942
Letter from John to say he is coming home on leave for a week. Hooray, quite excited, also a letter from George, very nice letter indeed but then they always are very good and give me great pleasure.

MARCH 1ST 1942
Getting ready for John coming home tomorrow, busy cooking etc.

MARCH 2ND 1942
The day has arrived for me to meet John and how excited I am. Met John at 1.15 – quite full up. He looked very well indeed and ran to meet me lke a schoolboy home for his holidays. Went in the evening to the Scala to see Lydia, *then spent a very nice evening. Dave came and fixed the wireless for me and John paid for it. Weather very cold.*

MARCH 9TH 1942
John returned to Tidworth at 12.15. I feel very lonely and miss him very much, but Syd and I had lunch at the Crown Hotel and then went to the Gaumont to see Sun Valley. *Home to tea and read before going on duty.*

MARCH 21ST 1942
Feel very lonely just on my own, shall be very thankful when this war is over and my boys are home again.

APRIL 3RD 1942
Had a lovely surprise when I got home off duty, two lovely letters and snaps from George. Feel quite bucked up. They certainly are a wonderful tonic to me.

APRIL 18TH 1942
Feel rather lonely tonight. Shall be glad when this war is over and please God my boys return for I am very lonely on my own, but then I know what my boys would say – 'Keep your chin up and don't worry, we'll be back with you soon and playing you up like old times'.

MAY 18TH 1942
Shall be glad when John is home again for his leave, another two weeks now then I shall see his dear old face again. Oh yes, the time when I have to meet my dear George – Oh God, how good that time will be when we three are together again and how I long for that time to come, please God all will be well.

JUNE 8TH 1942
Letter from John, he is coming home in a fortnight's time, passed his wireless examinations, going on Friday to Castle Martin – hope he will like it there and be alright.

JUNE 26TH 1942
Well, I have had a big surprise and very pleased too. John has arrived unexpectedly for fourteen days, so shall have my holiday too. He looks fit and well.

For the next fourteen days the diary records how John and mother spent their days together – visiting friends and his employer, going to cinemas and shopping.

JULY 7TH 1942
John busy packing and getting ready for his journey tomorrow. I shall miss him very much indeed. But thank God we have had a very enjoyable time.

JULY 9TH 1942
The morning has arrived for John to return. Went to see him off. I feel very full up.

JULY 20TH 1942
No letters from John or George so expect John is on his way somewhere, please God will protect him and keep him safe.

JULY 23RD 1942
No letters from boys. Have written a note to Syd to attend to everything while my boys are abroad should anything happen to me.

JULY 27TH 1942
Came off duty at 10pm. Went to bed and woke to noise of planes. Jerries, very bad raid indeed. Just went up the garden and had to duck as I heard one coming. It landed in Rookery Road by Purus so went round to the post to help with the wounded until 7.30. Then had a rest and went up to town shopping. The glass is out again in the French windows and plenty of dirt. Just had lunch and started cleaning up. Five Ways, Vicarage Road, Hockley, Stratford Road, Sutton, Sherlock Street, in fact all round Birmingham. Bordesley Green, Moor Street, Woolworth's and Peark's on Soho Road burnt out. Also Lewis's Repository still burning at 1400 hours. Raid started at 1.40 – all clear at 5.30. Letter from George, very good tonic after night of hell.

JULY 30TH 1942
Sirens at 1.45am; hardly got cap on when casualties arrived, nearly all AFS or firefighters, wardens – wounds from incendiaries exploding. Very bad night again and we were very busy. Felt tired out so went to bed for a few hours. On duty tonight at 10pm. Sirens 12.45, all clear 3.15. No casualties. Got shelter ready.

AUGUST 4TH 1942
Purple warning at 2.13-2.47am. Came off duty but feel things are not so good. I do so wish this war was over, nothing but worry and wondering, and home to such a lonely place without my boys.

AUGUST 19TH 1942
A letter from John but no date or place mentioned so don't know where he is, or where he is going.

AUGUST 28TH 1942
Night off but didn't sleep – planes going over. I think my nerves are run down for I can't bear the noise of the planes.

AUGUST 31ST 1942
Great surprise. Telegram from John with message but no address – touched me greatly, had to shed a few tears but thank God he has landed safely somewhere.

SEPTEMBER 10TH 1942
Airgraph letter from John – he is still on his journey but in good health and spirits.

SEPTEMBER 11TH 1942
Sitting in garden reading and thinking of my two boys, and longing for

their return.

SEPTEMBER 15TH 1942
Oh this terrible war. I wish it was over so as we could all be at peace again – it gets on one's nerves. War, war, war. Always living in dread of raids. I must dry up or else I shall think I'm getting nervy.

OCTOBER 5TH 1942
Glorious surprise. Letter from John – he is in Egypt. Feel much better now I have heard from him.

NOVEMBER 26TH 1942
Airgraph from John and he has received some of my letters. He is in Alexandria.

JANUARY 4TH 1943
Telegram from George to say that John was OK, also a letter dated 19/7/42, nearly five months. No news from John yet.

The rest of the diary is in a similar vein. With her two boys abroad she records her innermost feelings, longing only for their safe return – many mothers must have felt the same. Each letter she received and sent is faithfully recorded in her daily entries.

The diary ended on March 9th 1944 when John came home from Italy to return to his Regiment in Worthing where they were preparing for the invasion of France. It was never continued.

Appendix B

List of soldiers of the 44th Royal Tank Regiment who gave their lives during the campaign in North West Europe. Extracted from the records of the Bevrijdingsmuseum, Groesbeek, The Netherlands – compiled by Jan Hey.

26.06.44 BATTLE P, Tpr......................................St-Manvieu War Cem., Cheux (F)
27.06.44 BRYANT J S M, Tpr ....St-Manvieu War Cem., Cheux (F)
27.06.44 COHEN C S, Tpr ....St-Manvieu War Cem., Cheux (F)
29.06.44 ANDERSON R, Tpr ....Banneville-la-Campagne War Cem. (F)
29.06.44 AXTELL E J, Tpr ....Missing in Action
29.06.44 BELL J E, L.Sjt ....Missing in Action
29.06.44 BROWNELL J, Tpr...............................Ryes War Cem., Bazenville (F)
29.06.44 CALLAGHAN E, Tpr............................Missing in Action
29.06.44 COLBECK-WELCH J C, Lt ....Banneville-la-Campagne War Cem. (F)
29.06.44 LAFFORD J, L.Cpl ....Missing in Action
29.06.44 LIVINGSTONE W W, Cpl...................Banneville-la-Campagne War Cem. (F)
29.06.44 MORTIMER R, Tpr ....Missing in Action
29.06.44 PATTINGALE R V, Tpr ....Brouay War Cem. (F)
29.06.44 RUMBLE J, Tpr....................................Hottot-les-Bagues War Cem. (F)
29.06.44 SINDEN K F, L.Cpl ....Banneville-la-Campagne War Cem. (F)
29.06.44 WALLER D, Tpr ....Missing in Action
29.06.44 WENSLEY R E G, Cpl..........................Missing in Action
30.06.44 THOMAS A D, Tpr..............................St Manvieu War Cem., Cheux (F)
13.07.44 CAMPBELL W G F, Tpr ....St Manvieu War Cem., Cheux (F)
17.07.44 NAYLOR F W, Tpr...............................Ryes War Cem., Bazenville (F)
21.07.44 KING C G, Tpr....................................Ryes War Cem., Bazenville (F)
06.08.44 BEEBE R, Tpr......................................Bayeux War Cem. (F)
07.08.44 PIPE A J H, Tpr ....St-Charles-de-Percy War Cem. (F)
07.08.44 SAVAGE G, L.Cpl................................St-Charles-de-Percy War Cem. (F)
07.08.44 THOMSON C D, Capt ....St-Charles-de-Percy War Cem. (F)
16.08.44 GUEST L J, Tpr....................................Ranville War Cem. (F)
16.08.44 RICHARDSON J G, Sjt........................Banneville-la-Campagne War Cem. (F)
18.08.44 DAVIES G, Tpr ....Banneville-la-Campagne War Cem. (F)
18.08.44 GALLAGHER P D, 2/Lt ....Banneville-la-Campagne War Cem. (F)
18.08.44 O'SHEA G M, Tpr...............................Banneville-la-Campagne War Cem. (F)
18.08.44 SHARP M F, Tpr..................................Banneville-la-Campagne War Cem. (F)
18.08.44 SOLE J E, Tpr ....Banneville-la-Campagne War Cem. (F)
18.08.44 UPSTONE L J, Tpr...............................Missing in Action
19.08.44 BURROW H D, Tpr.............................Banneville-la-Campagne War Cem. (F)
19.08.44 ELLAM F, Sjt..Banneville-la-Campagne War Cem. (F)
02.09.44 PORTNER W H, Tpr
              (served as Porter).................Canaples Churchyard (Somme) (F)
06.09.44 ROTHWELL J, Tpr...............................Leopoldsburg War Cem. (B)
07.09.44 HURST R, Tpr......................................Heverlee War Cem. (B)

Date	Name	Cemetery
07.09.44	KENWAY R A, Sjt	Heverlee War Cem. (B)
07.09.44	LOBB R, WO.II(SSM)	Heverlee War Cem. (B)
07.09.44	MARLEY J, Tpr	Heverlee War Cem. (B)
07.09.44	OSBORNE G S, Lt	Leopoldsburg War Cem. (B)
07.09.44	PARTRIDGE G T, Tpr	Brugge General Cem. (B)
07.09.44	SPANNER P, Tpr	Heverlee War Cem. (B)
07.09.44	THOMAS K, L.Cpl	Leopoldsburg War Cem. (B)
07.09.44	WILLIAMS L L, Tpr	Waregem Communal Cem. (B)
20.09.44	NICHOLLS B, Tpr	Mierlo War Cem. (NL)
20.09.44	STOTHARD R, Cpl	Mierlo War Cem. (NL)
21.09.44	MATTHEWS S, Tpr	Uden War Cem. (NL)
21.09.44	THOROGOOD J F, Tpr	Uden War Cem. (NL)
22.09.44	CLAYTON W H, Tpr	Leopoldsburg War Cem. (B)
22.09.44	COOPER A J, Tpr	Missing in Action
24.09.44	ANDERSON J, Tpr	Missing in Action
24.09.44	ASTIN G L, Tpr	Veghel (Eerde) RC Cem. (NL)
24.09.44	HARDY J E, Tpr	Veghel (Eerde) RC Cem. (NL)
24.09.44	HOOPER W R, Lt	Veghel (Eerde) RC Cem. (NL)
24.09.44	JONES J, Tpr	Veghel (Eerde) RC Cem. (NL)
24.09.44	STACEY F W, Tpr	Veghel (Eerde) RC Cem. (NL)
25.09.44	HARMAN F A, Tpr	Uden War Cem. (NL)
25.09.44	HOLLIS P C, Tpr	Uden War Cem. (NL)
25.09.44	HUGGINS F H, Tpr	Uden War Cem. (NL)
25.09.44	NEWMAN T, L.Sjt	Uden War Cem. (NL)
25.09.44	ROBINSON W, Tpr	Uden War Cem. (NL)
25.09.44	WORLEY W W, L.Sjt	Uden War Cem. (NL)
26.10.44	LEAVER M C R, Tpr	Leopoldsburg War Cem. (B)
26.10.44	LEE S, Tpr	Leopoldsburg War Cem. (B)
25.11.44	PALFREY F R, Tpr	Brussel Town Cem. (B)
29.11.44	BROOKS A, Tpr	Valkenswaard War Cem. (NL)
29.11.44	JOHNSON E L, Lt	Valkenswaard War Cem. (NL)
29.11.44	LOCKEY R A, 2/Lt	Valkenswaard War Cem. (NL)
29.11.44	MILNE E F W, Tpr	Valkenswaard War Cem. (NL)
01.02.45	ELLERBY R, Tpr	Hull Northern Cem., (UK)
27.02.45	BARLOW N W, L.Sjt	Kleve War Cem. (D)
27.02.45	SLANN E L, Tpr	Kleve War Cem. (D)
27.02.45	WICKHAM W G J, Tpr	Kleve War Cem. (D)
28.02.45	LANGWORTHY W J G, Sjt	Kleve War Cem. (D)
01.03.45	ANDERSON I C, Tpr	Kleve War Cem. (D)
01.03.45	ARMSTRONG-WHITWORTH K B A, Tpr	Kleve War Cem. (D)
01.03.45	CAMPBELL G W, Tpr	Kleve War Cem. (D)
01.03.45	RAMSEY H P, Cpl	Kleve War Cem. (D)
02.03.45	HAMILTON J P, Lt	Kleve War Cem. (D)
02.03.45	USHER E C, Cpl	Kleve War Cem. (D)

24.03.45	ANSON M L, Cpl	Missing in Action
24.03.45	THOM G, L.Sjt	Venray War Cem. (NL)
25.03.45	CHAPMAN L B, Lt	Kleve War Cem. (D)
25.03.45	COLLEY M, Cpl	Eindhoven (Woensel) Gen. Cem. (NL)
25.03.45	JOY W G, L.Cpl	Kleve War Cem. (D)
25.03.45	KENT D, Tpr	Kleve War Cem. (D)
25.03.45	WHITE H W, Tpr	Kleve War Cem. (D)
28.03.45	DAVIES J A, Tpr	Kleve War Cem. (D)
28.03.45	SHAW B, L.Sjt	Kleve War Cem. (D)
29.03.45	WALPOLE R H, Tpr	Venray War Cem. (NL)
09.04.45	EVANS W L, Lt	Rheinberg War Cem. (D)
14.04.45	HOLDEN K J, Tpr	Becklingen War Cem. (D)
18.04.45	BATHAM K A, Lt	Becklingen War Cem. (D)
18.04.45	BORTHWICK J S, Tpr	Missing in Action
19.04.45	LOWE J H, Tpr	Becklingen War Cem. (D)
26.04.45	AUDSLEY J W, Tpr	Becklingen War Cem. (D)
19.06.45	ARMSTRONG G T, Tpr	Hannover War Cem. (D)
02.07.45	SWAIN A J, L.Cpl	Kiel War Cem. (D)
08.05.45	JOHNSON W A, Sjt	Hannover War Cem. (D)
19.03.45	WATKINS W J B, Capt	Bristol (Canford) Cem. (UK)
15.11.45	MILLICHAMP A E, L.Cpl	Aylesford Cem. (UK)
12.12.45	BURKE T, Tpr	Glasgow (St Peter's) RC Cem. (UK)